Small Groups Growing Churches

**training dynamic leaders for
today's needs and tomorrow's challenges**

MIKE LAW

SMALL GROUPS GROWING CHURCHES

About the author: Mike Law is the administrator of the Christian Resources Project (14 Lipson Road, Plymouth, PL4 8PW), a registered charity he founded over twenty years ago. He is actively involved in schools ministry, running a resource centre, preaching and teaching. Following a number of years in which he was an associate (volunteer) trainer with Scripture Union, he has been devising and running training courses for youth and children's workers and for small group leaders. He has led all sorts of small groups and claims to have been involved in more committees than are good for any sane person! He is a member of Mutley Baptist Church in Plymouth where he is an elder with specific responsibility for oversight of the children's work.

Published by Scripture Union, 207–209 Queensway, Bletchley, MK2 2EB, England.

Scripture Union: We are an international Christian charity working with churches in more than 130 countries providing resources to bring the good news about Jesus Christ to children, young people and families – and to encourage them to develop spiritually through the Bible and prayer. As well as our network of volunteers, staff and associates who run holidays, church-based events and school Christian groups, we produce a wide range of publications and support those who use our resources through training programmes.

Email: info@scriptureunion.org.uk
Internet: www.scriptureunion.org.uk

British Library Cataloguing-in-Publication Data: a catalogue record for this book is available from the British Library.

Quotations from John Stott (chapter 4), Chris Fabry (chapter 6), E P Clowney (chapter 8), Nick Pollard (chapter 10), Jon Bush (chapter 15) all gratefully used with permission.

Scripture taken from THE MESSAGE © Eugene H Peterson, 1993, 1994, 1995. Used by permission of NavPress Publishing Group.

Scripture taken from THE HOLY BIBLE, NEW INTERNATIONAL VERSION © 1973, 1978, 1984 by International Bible Society. Anglicisation © 1979, 1984, 1989. Used by permission of Hodder and Stoughton Ltd.

Cover design by David Lund Design, Milton Keynes.
Cover cartoon and internal illustrations by Fred Chevalier, Worcester.
Internal design and typesetting by Servis Filmsetting Ltd, Manchester.
Printed and bound in Malta by Interprint Limited.

Contents

Welcome!

What makes churches grow? A survey published in the *UK Christian Handbook Religious Trends 3* lists eight factors, one of which is 'holistic small groups'. Good small groups are an integral factor in growing churches – and this manual will help any church grow good groups through the training of effective group leaders. It's a book of small group studies with a difference! It's designed specifically for the people who lead small groups – often struggling with little or no training and few resources. And apparently there's an absolute army of you out there – recent statistics show that UK churches have a staggering 200,000 small groups.

One of the best ways of training small group leaders is *in* a small group setting. Not only can leaders learn new ideas and skills, but they actually have a chance to work them out in a real small group situation.

The material here can be used:

- **consecutively as a comprehensive training course** – spread over fifteen weeks, each chapter provides the basis for one training session. For training new leaders from scratch this is probably the best method.
- **on a one-off basis** – choose particular topics you wish to cover and use the relevant chapter. This is best suited for an established team of leaders wishing to refresh their skills.
- **to create a one day or weekend training course** – select the topics you want to cover according to the number of sessions you are able to include in your programme.

Most studies contain enough material for a meeting of about one and a half to two hours. If the time you have available is less than this, select the material you find most helpful or use the material over more than one session.

These group studies are intended for groups of leaders working together to improve their skills. They are not intended to be used as complete studies within home groups. However, the techniques and individual parts of the studies can – and should – be transplanted into your small group programme.

Whichever way you organise your training, it will be helpful if all leaders have their own copy of the book to read. And don't forget – whether you use all or just some of the material, a coffee break with time to relax and chat is an essential part of any training experience!

Those on the training course will need to develop the ability to think about two situations at the same time. There is always more than one group in focus; the group of leaders who are being trained and the groups that those leaders lead. Some questions will relate more easily to one than the other and this should be reasonably obvious. If in doubt, consider both groups. Where leaders being trained do not currently lead, or have never led a group, then they need to reflect on a group they have been a part of, or on the group they expect to lead.

Each chapter starts with an overview of the topic. This highlights some of the main issues. The **Ideas** section gives a range of suggestions for activities which can be used in small groups. These can be incorporated into your training course or simply left for leaders to try out in their own groups.

The **GROUP FOCUS** section looks at one aspect of small group life and explores what the Bible has to say about it. In doing so, it uses a wide variety of techniques – more than you would normally use in a small group – in order to demonstrate methods which can be used when leaders go back to their own groups. Most **GROUP FOCUS** sections do not require much more in the way of equipment than Bible, pen and paper. Occasionally other items are necessary, so read through the study first and note anything you need to provide. One thing which occurs frequently is 'a large sheet of paper'. This needs to be big enough for several people (equipped with felt-tip pens) to work on at the same time. An A1 flip chart pad or something larger would be fine. You could use it on an easel, or put it on a table or just lay it on the floor – watching out that pens don't bleed through onto the carpet!

There are specific chapters covering the topics of worship and prayer. It will be helpful for the person organising the training to read these chapters and then to incorporate some of the ideas and techniques wherever worship and prayer are suggested in the various **GROUP FOCUS** times.

Sections headed **Reflect** and **Review** occur at various points in the book. **Reflect** provides an opportunity to assess where you are personally. **Review** suggests ways in which you can think through techniques and ideas and apply them to the group, together in the training group or on your own. The **Takeaway** section is for you to consider which ideas and techniques could be transferred to the group you lead or will be leading. Don't skip over these sections. They're potentially the most important elements of the whole book.

The **To think about . . .** slot is self-explanatory! But don't just read it and pass on. Take a few moments to ask:

- What is the author trying to say?
- Why has it been included at this point?
- What ideas for further thought and exploration does it give me?

The occasional **Diary** is intended to hold a mirror up to the peculiar ways we think and act. Enjoy and consider!

The chapters do not follow a logically planned theme from point A to point Z. Rather, they operate as a compendium of ideas, techniques, thoughts and inspirations. They will only work if they are tried out. **This is not the sort of book you can just sit and read. Unless you experience the studies and try the ideas you will lose most of the value of the book.**

By the way, the words 'small group', 'housegroup' and 'home group' are used interchangeably and are meant to be widely inclusive of all kinds of small-scale gatherings operating within churches of all denominations.

Resources

Resources specific to the different topics are listed in each chapter but the following titles cover a range of topics. Throughout the book the selection is personal. They are mostly books I have read, used and valued, and any recommendations are genuine.

Housegroups Eds. Ian Coffey and Stephen Gaukroger. Crossway Books (IVP). Subtitled 'The leaders' survival guide', this is a good introduction to most areas of housegroup life.

The Small Group Leader John Mallinson. Scripture Union. No, not for leaders who are only four feet tall! This is the classic book on leading small groups in the church, covering all aspects from setting up groups to bringing them to an end.

Small Group Know How Bryn Hughes. Monarch. Looks at understanding groups, leading groups and leadership skills.

50 Ways to Help Your Church Grow David Beer. Kingsway. Not specifically about small groups but useful reading to help small group leaders think about the larger church picture.

Grove Books publish a large series of 24-page booklets covering a huge variety of topics, divided into seven series: Biblical, Ethical, Evangelism, Pastoral, Renewal, Spirituality and Worship. The books are inexpensive and new titles are regularly published. Write for a catalogue to Grove Books Ltd., Ridley Hall Road, Cambridge, CB3 9HU. Or contact sales@grovebooks.co.uk

It's likely you will find that some of the recommended books are already out of print. Others will inevitably go out of print during the lifetime of this book. But it's still worth making an effort to track them down. Your local library should be able to help. They can search other libraries around the country, and usually charge only a modest fee. Or try the Internet.

www.abebooks.com is a site which links a large number of secondhand booksellers around the world and allows you to search for titles and then order online.

Still on the subject of resources, you can't give consistently good output if you are not receiving good input. Some of this will come from sermons and teaching in the church, but leaders need to take the initiative to feed themselves. I strongly recommend that leaders find time to read (half an hour less TV?) and build up their own library of useful books. However, books are expensive. It's a good idea for the church to buy books which can be circulated among leaders. Don't put them on a shelf and call them a library – no one will ever go near them! Take time in training sessions to recommend books that will really repay time spent reading.

A few useful websites:

www.scriptureunion.org.uk
www.ivpbooks.com
www.christianresourceproject.org.uk
www.christian-aid.org.uk
www.alphacourse.org
www.abebooks.com
www.amazon.co.uk

Entering 'Christian small groups resources' into a search engine will produce a large number of interesting sites.

Finally, keep an ideas file or folder to supplement this book or jot things down in the margins. You'll be amazed how often it provides just the inspiration you need.

Getting from A to B – or not!
During the editing process it was suggested that each chapter of this book should have a clearly defined aim printed at the start. An aim says, 'We are at A and we want to get to B – this will help us to do it.' But I don't know where you are starting from; what knowledge and experience you are bringing to the book. Nor do I know your companions for the journey; the small group you will be part of as you work through this material. So rather than help you move from an 'A' that I've determined (and where you may not be!) to an equally determined 'B' (where you may not want to go!), each chapter is designed to have a wide range of inputs in all sorts of different forms so that within it you can find your own starting point and a finishing point that's helpful to you. One advantage of this approach is that you can come back to the material more than once and find that it will guide you on a variety of journeys.

In a nutshell, the aims of the book are:

- to help broaden your thinking and understanding of a variety of issues relating to small groups;
- to provide materials for small group experiences which will both help in your journey and provide models you can use in helping others;
- to encourage you to get into the habit of reflecting – on your own and with a group – about what you've learned, the way in which you have learned it and how these things can be applied to the groups you lead.

1 Leading the Way

The qualities of a good small group leader

What is a leader? Someone who leads. Well, not quite. A leader is someone who leads in such a way that others follow. Think about some of the groups, inside and outside the church, that you have been part of. How often have you been in groups where one person has been appointed as leader but someone else has been the one everyone listens to, everyone follows?

What makes a leader a LEADER?

- **Personality**   Some people are just naturally better leaders than others. If you're very shy, find it difficult to hold a conversation and can't organise the proverbial drinks party, then you're probably not cut out to be a leader.
- **Integrity**   Being a person of your word. Not favouring one member of the group over another. A good match between the way you live and the things you say.
- **Relationship**   Knowing and being known by members of the group. Being ready to listen, to give time to people and to care.
- **Knowledge**   This is different from being 'a know-all'. A good leader has taken time beforehand to master the subject, whether it's a Bible study or the agenda of the drains committee.

Reflect

Do others see me as a leader? What evidence do I have that others follow my lead?

Can you learn leadership or is it a gift?   You can definitely learn a whole range of skills a good leader needs:

- how to be a good listener
- how to be disciplined in preparation
- how to handle difficulties that arise in the group
- how to know when you're out of your depth and what to do about it

How do you learn? Here are some strategies:

Thinking things through   When you've led a group, take time to think through what happened. What could you have done better? What other ways could you have led the group? What different techniques could you have used? What difference would these have made? Don't get negative about it, but always look for ways you can improve. Find a trusted and wise friend who can observe you in action and help you reflect. It's probably not a good idea to ask the group as a whole to reflect on your leadership. You will either get a lot of very nice things said – very encouraging but not very helpful – or you will find everybody has a different opinion. If they really think you're a terrible leader, you will pick this up without having to ask them.

Studying   At your own pace and as you have time, read books and articles about leadership. Find out about different techniques which can be used to change the way the group functions.

Observing   Look at the way other people lead groups. Make a mental note of their strengths and weaknesses. Think about how *you* would have led the group.

Taking time   You can't build good relationships just in the time you're together as a group. Take an interest in people *outside* of group meetings. You don't have to go round to visit everyone (though sometimes a visit might be helpful) but make sure you don't ignore people if you meet them in the supermarket or over coffee after the church service.

Praying   Basic but necessary. Pray simply but genuinely for each member of the group; every day, every week; whatever is appropriate.

Being aware of what's going on in the world   What's happening in the news? What are the issues people are concerned about?

Reflect

What am I doing to improve my leadership skills?

Under authority   The centurion who asks Jesus to help his servant (Matthew 8:5–13) gives us a great picture of Christian leadership. 'I myself am a man under authority, with soldiers under me.' His authority as a centurion came from the authority of those above him; ultimately the emperor himself. A good leader is someone under authority.

Under the authority of the church leadership   Good leaders do not criticise the minister, rubbish the deacons or the PCC or go against decisions taken by the church. That doesn't mean leaders cannot disagree with other leaders but they do it in a considerate and thoughtful way, face to face, not by leading a group which is hostile and critical.

Under the authority of God   The key to all Christian leadership is a personal relationship with God. Leaders are not necessarily more spiritual or better Christians than others in the church, but they have particular responsibilities and need to depend on God to meet them. Leaders need to be regular at services and prayer meetings and consistent in maintaining and developing their own personal devotional and study life.

(More about study in chapter 4.) If you don't have time to do these things, you don't have time to be a leader. And if you think it doesn't really matter, take a look at Luke 20:45–47 and James 3:1 to see the dangers.

Reflect

Who are the leaders in authority over me? How good am I as a follower?

It's great!   Just in case you're beginning to despair and to think 'Is it all worth it?' there are great rewards from being a leader! There's nothing to compare to the thrill of seeing that God has used you to do something special for him.

Ideas

Read biographies of famous leaders. Your local library will have plenty. Make a note of characteristics you might copy, and those best avoided.

Follow, in more than one newspaper, a current news story featuring a leading politician. Try to build up a profile of her/his style of leadership, strengths and weaknesses. What would you do differently?

At the next committee meeting you attend, focus all your attention on listening. Speak only if asked a direct question. Afterwards ask yourself:

- How did it feel?
- How did others react?
- What did you learn?

Check out your style of leadership. Mark an X on the line showing where you fit between the two extremes.

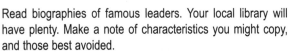

pastor		prophet
listener		speaker
thinker		doer
conservative		radical
pragmatist		idealist

Look at areas where you have marked yourself strongly to one side or the other. How can you strengthen the weaker side and provide balance in your leadership?

On a large sheet of paper, use a chart like this to help you plan your progress as a leader.

	In my personal life	As a leader training with others	As a leader of my small group
Where am I now?			
What do I hope to achieve in the next year?			
What help/resources do I need?			
Where do I find help/resources?			
What are my prayer needs?			
Who will pray for me?			

GROUP FOCUS

Who will lead this session?   Divide the material you are going to use into four parts and choose a different leader for each part. These leaders should be people who are broad shouldered enough to accept criticism and willing to learn from it because, at the end of the session, you will think about the different ways each person led.

Brainstorm: Which leader in world history (excluding Jesus):

- was the most powerful?
- had the greatest effect on civilisation?
- do you most admire?

Go round the group sharing examples of leaders (teachers, youth leaders, ministers . . .) who have significantly affected your life. Take time to thank God for these people.

On a large sheet of paper draw two columns and list the characteristics of good leadership and bad leadership which have emerged so far in your discussions. Keep the list because you'll be adding to it throughout the session.

Divide the group into four smaller groups (pairs are OK), each looking at one of the following passages:

Joshua 1:1–9
Matthew 23
John 13:1–17
1 Timothy 3:1–12

From these passages add to the lists of features of good leadership and bad leadership. Look at the lists you have drawn up. Discuss together anything you don't understand or anything you disagree with.

As a group, decide on three good characteristics which are particularly important for a small group leader and three characteristics from the 'bad' column which provide relevant warnings for small group leaders.

The two letters to Timothy are full of practical advice from an older leader (Paul) to a younger one (Timothy). Read both letters straight through individually – it only takes about 15 minutes. Then go through section by section as a whole group, looking out for what Paul says about:

- false teaching
- prayer
- relationships between leaders and people
- personal spiritual growth
- coping with difficulties
- Scripture
- Jesus

Imagine you are putting together one of those 'mini' books so popular in gift shops. This one is called *Top Tips from Timothy*. On facing pages you have a verse (or part of one) from 1 or 2 Timothy and on the opposite page a short (witty?) saying. Try to create pages for the seven topics above. One example:

For God did not give us a spirit of timidity but a spirit of power, of love and of self-discipline.
2 Tim 1:7

Don't be afraid to
- love
- learn
- lead

In pairs share one thing you have learned about leadership and yourself. Finish the session by praying for one another, still in pairs.

Review

Go round the group and ask each member to make one positive comment about the way each of the four leaders has run their part of the group. Then ask each of the four leaders to mention one particular difficulty they found when leading, or one thing they would do differently another time.

Resources

Capture Your Call Terry Anne Preston. Bible Reading Fellowship. A series of studies focussing on how we can hear the call of God. Contains useful charts for discovering what area of service God is calling you into.

Grow Your Own Leaders Anton Baumohl. Scripture Union. A practical guide to training in the local church.

Calling Christian Leaders John Stott. IVP. Biblical models of church, gospel and ministry.

The Sacred Diary of Adrian Plass Adrian Plass. Marshall Pickering. If you think you've got problems, then read what happens to Adrian Plass after he becomes a study group leader!

The 77 Habits of Highly Ineffective Christians Chris Fabry. Intervarsity Press. Amusing, thought-provoking and challenging.

The **Dilbert** cartoon books Scott Adams. Andrews McMeel Publishing. Widely available in secular bookshops. Although incredibly cynical, they will provide many insights into the problems of leadership and being led. See also www.dilbert.com

To think about . . .

'When a blind man leads a blind man, they both end up in the ditch.' Matthew 15:14. *The Message*

Reflect

What have I learned in this session about:

- what makes a good leader?
- my strengths as a leader?
- my weaknesses as a leader?
- the way I related to others in the group?
- the things I find difficult in a group situation?

Takeaway

What techniques from the group time could I effectively use in my small group?

Diary

Week 1 – They're a funny lot, these other housegroup leaders. Not sure all of them are Christians. Some of them don't have a daily quiet time! Mind you, one or two are too keen. When I mentioned I'd overslept this morning and hadn't had time to read the Bible, you'd have thought I'd committed the unforgivable sin.

Week 2 – Thought the session Sheila led was very thought-provoking. Of course, I wouldn't do it that way. But I could see that it might get round some of the barriers people hide behind in housegroups.

Week 3 – I've always thought the leader's job was to keep the group strictly to the task and make sure they came up with the right answers to the questions. But, I have to admit, when it was my turn to lead tonight, the path we travelled was not the one I'd planned and the 'right' answers turned out to be quite different from what I'd expected!

2 Coming Together

Purposes, practicalities, and people problems

If you've ever tried to decide at a church meeting of 70 people of different ages and backgrounds what colour the church china should be; or tried to plan a 'Churches Together' communion service in a group representing Brethren, Anglicans, Roman Catholics and Salvation Army, then you'll have discovered that different sorts of groups are best suited to different sorts of purposes!

What is the purpose of the group? A committee planning building work may need to be composed of very similar people, all with specific qualifications and experience. A group reflecting on the worship life of the church will probably need to contain a very wide cross section of different people. The purpose of the group ideally defines its membership. When we've decided on the purpose we can go on to consider:

- what kind of group will best fulfil this purpose?
- how do we create such a group?
- how often should they meet and where?
- what should be the structure of their meetings?

Sometimes the purpose of a group is taken for granted. This is often the case with housegroups. What results is that one person goes to the group looking for 'in-depth Bible study', another for 'a bit of fellowship', another for 'somewhere I can share my ideas instead of just listening to the sermon' and others to meet a wide variety of needs. Inevitably, most will end up disappointed. Housegroups will often have a mix of purposes, but it is helpful to list them (in order of priority if possible) and then begin to work out how they can be fulfilled. Here are some possible purposes and some of the initial questions to be considered:

- **Studying the Bible together:** Who will lead? What material?
- **Building relationships:** Who will be in which group? What if people don't get on?
- **Prayer:** For what? How long? How can we learn to pray better?
- **Pastoral Care:** Who is responsible? How does this group relate to rest of church?

We shall look at some of these issues in more detail later, but the important thing is to realise that they need to be considered **before** a new group is started. Where groups already exist they need to be incorporated into any review of groups.

Reflect

Do the groups I am part of have a clear purpose that everyone understands?

Pity about the people! Ever thought your group would be great if it wasn't for the people who belong to it? Just imagine . . .

Tom is a lovely chap. Eighty-six years old. Been a mis-sionary most of his life and still goes round preaching in old people's homes (well, he doesn't think of *himself* as old). He knows there are only two ways of doing things; his way and the wrong way.

Wayne is a really enthusiastic 18-year-old, recently converted and absolutely full of it. He has a dozen new ideas every week and thinks the group should try them all out at once.

Sarah is middle-aged, very loyal, a serious Christian but painfully shy. Unfortunately, when anyone tries to draw her out by asking her a question she replies in such an irrelevant way that everyone is left completely baffled.

Rohan works in management, always on some new training course. He realises the group leader doesn't know nearly as much about leading a group as he does, but he doesn't want to make a direct challenge . . . so he tries out different *techniques* he has learned on the group.

Mavis just says what she thinks – usually *without* thinking about it.

And so we could go on. How are these people going to change from being a collection of individuals to a functioning group?

Work at growing trust There need to be ground rules about:

- confidentiality
- listening while others speak
- not being critical of others in the group
- agreeing to pray for one another in between meetings

Take time Individuals and groups change slowly – and the more diverse the group the longer it will take to gel. As a leader, take time to get to know each member of the group individually. Find out their interests; what makes them tick. Be concerned about their concerns; be interested in their interests. A friend of mine asked a group of mature ladies in a Bible study group to talk about their childhood and teenage years, expecting mainly pleasant memories. She was amazed how many had been through major tragedy and trauma. Although members of the group knew each other reasonably well, these disclosures came as a great surprise. There is *always* more to people's lives and experiences than meets the eye.

Be tactful and sensitive This applies especially to encouraging the over-talkative to speak less and the shyer members to contribute.

Create opportunities for reflection Give the group time to reflect on their development and growth and suggest ways things can be improved.

Create opportunities for socialising The group will benefit from meeting outside the normal framework; for a meal or an outing or tackling a work project.

When you've done all you can, accept the facts that some groups will never gel. It may be necessary to ask people to change to another group where they will be more at home (or less of a disruption!).

Reflect

Who are the people I lead? What are their strengths? What are their needs? How am I working to build a group?

Practical points about meeting together

- If you meet in someone's home, take care not to impose too much of a burden. Give thought to how tea, coffee and food are provided. Should different people bring something each week? Or what about a box for members to make contributions towards costs? Don't assume the host can cover everything. And make sure there's help with the washing up!
- If you meet in a church, try to make the venue as suitable as possible for your group. A business meeting might require sitting around a table. A Bible study or prayer meeting probably won't.
- If you have to meet as a small group in a large room try to create an area in the room which can be more intimate.
- When members are absent, tactfully find out why. Nobody wants to feel nagged, but they don't like to feel unmissed either.

Review

How well do the practical arrangements for the group work? What are the sticky points?

Ideas

Social activities Try some of the following:

- **Bowling** Great fun whether at the local Superbowl or a skittle alley in a pub.
- **Eat together** In a home, on a picnic, at a restaurant. What about a serial meal where you eat starters at one person's home, main course at another and so on through as many courses as you want until coffee?
- **Go to the cinema** There's not much fellowship sitting in the dark but there is in discussing the film over a drink afterwards.
- **Take on a job together** Working on a common task – decorating someone's home or DIY at the church, digging a garden, organising a meal for, say, asylum seekers – can be one of the best ways of helping the group grow together.
  What about a **pizza and video** night?

Draw up a group covenant This can include simple agreements like keeping things confidential, arriving on time, sending apologies when absent, through to things like committing to pray for one another regularly, being willing to listen to others and being willing to accept when others challenge my beliefs, value and behaviour. There's information about group covenants in *The Small Group Leader* (see Resources page 6) and *Search the Scriptures* (see Resources below). *The Small Group Leader* also has a good selection of ideas for 'Get-acquainted Exercises'.

Draw up *The Ten Commandments for Small Groups* Make a list of the things you all think are important. Get someone with artistic skills or someone who is computer literate to produce them as a poster or as a card which could be kept in a wallet.

There are more ideas in chapter 7.

GROUP FOCUS

Use the **Working Together Board Game** at the end of the chapter. This is a different way to work together as a group, and particularly helpful when dealing with a daunting amount of Bible text. It might be easier if you photocopy the page to an enlarged A3 size. Sometimes the answers will be very brief. Sometimes there will be a lot to discuss. It may be helpful if one person keeps notes of the points raised. Afterwards re-read the notes. Try to find at least three practical things you can do as a group to help you work together and grow together more effectively.

Resources

Six of the *Serendipity* Bible study books originally brought to Britain from the US in the 1980s have been updated and re-published by Scripture Union under the series title of ***Bodybuilders***. The material is very good for new groups seeking to establish themselves and build good relationships. The titles available are:

Living for the King 'Tricia Williams
Surviving Under Pressure Christopher Griffiths and Stephen Hathway
A Fresh Encounter David Bolster
Relationship Building Lance Pierson
Growing Through Change Lance Pierson
Designed for Great Things Anton Baumohl

Also look out for: *Search the Scriptures* Lyman Coleman. Serendipity House. This is the original book, which is packed with useful ideas and techniques. And **Youth Ministry Resource Book** Lyman Coleman. Scripture Union. Similar to the above books. Although designed for young people's groups, much of the material is more widely applicable.

To think about . . .

The people I meet with – with all their funny habits and peculiar ways – are people for whom Christ died; my adopted family; the people with whom I will share eternity.

Reflect

How could I describe the purpose of my small group in a single sentence? What are the next three things I need to try in order to move towards meeting that purpose? How can I be more organised in praying for the members of my group?

Takeaway

Could I use the board game technique in my small group? Would my group have problems with using a board game and dice as part of a Bible study?

Diary

Week 1 – Don't know what we're trying to achieve in this group. I think it just exists because our minister went on a conference where they said small groups were a good thing.

Week 2 – Well, nothing special about small groups! All we did was study the Bible and pray together. Could do that anywhere. It was interesting to hear Jo's comments, though. There never used to be time for discussion when we had the old type of church Bible study.

Week 3 – It's a bit of a struggle with some people. But it was good to be able to pray for Sam. And I never knew that Sunita had been through so much. Surprising what you learn. Bit surprised about what I was prepared to tell them about me too!

The Working together board game!

Each player throws a dice and moves on her/his counter
— All the passages are from **Matthew**'s Gospel —

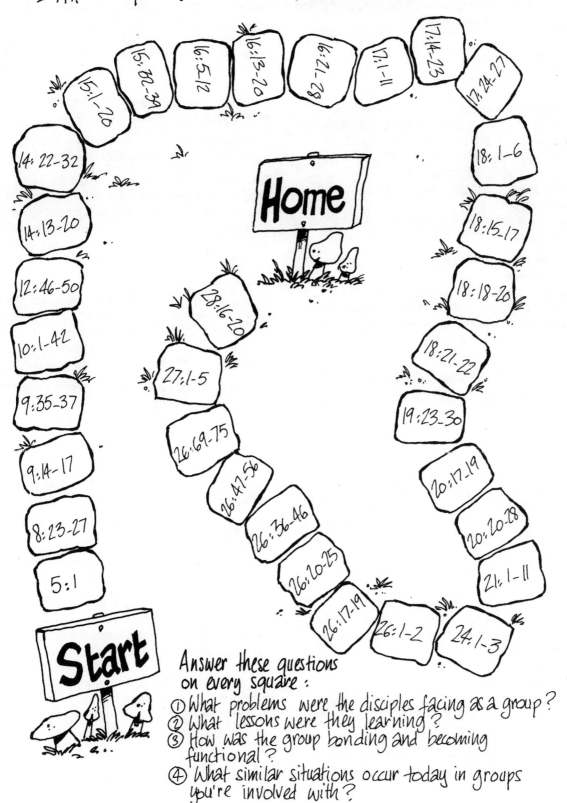

Answer these questions
on every square:

① What problems were the disciples facing as a group?
② What lessons were they learning?
③ How was the group bonding and becoming functional?
④ What similar situations occur today in groups you're involved with?

3 Into the Bible

God's Word: modelling, encouraging understanding, and using

There are lots of useful things small groups could do, so why spend time studying the Bible? After all, people are encouraged to read their own Bibles regularly. And they listen to sermons in church which teach the Bible. So, why use the Bible in groups?

Why the Bible?

- because the Bible is the Word of God. It's the main way God teaches us, rebukes us, corrects us and trains us to live the way he wants (2 Timothy 3:16).
- because trying to live a Christian life and ignoring the Bible is like going on a journey and ignoring the map. You may think you know the way, but sooner or later you take a wrong turn and get lost.
- because you can't share with others what you don't know for yourself.
- because studying the Bible is interesting, challenging, scary, exciting, fulfilling and fun!

Why study the Bible in small groups?   Critics say that Bible study in small groups is simply a sharing of ignorance – and sometimes they're right. Unpacking the meaning of a difficult passage of Scripture takes hard work, knowledge and experience. That's why good preachers spend many hours each week preparing that simple 25-minute sermon. The real strengths of small group studies lie not in unpacking deep theology but:

- applying the teaching of the Bible to everyday life. The small group setting provides opportunities to explore what this passage of Scripture means to *me* in *my* situation today.
- giving an opportunity to hear other people's experiences of trying to live out what they believe and supporting one another in it. Someone might say 'that's not Bible study – that's fellowship or pastoral care'. Bible study starts with understanding in the mind but it goes on to application in the life. Without both elements it's not real study. It's like watching all the cookery programmes on TV but living on junk food!
- giving an opportunity to ask questions and express doubts.
- creating an opportunity to hear from God.
- creating confidence in handling the Bible; confidence that will be valuable in sharing the good news with others outside the group.

Reflect

What part does the Bible play in my small group? Is our study of the Bible intellectual, practical or both?

The Bible and leading groups   There is one simple rule which can't be avoided or ignored: if you want to lead other people deeper into the Bible you must be going deeper into the Bible yourself. You may have lots of knowledge gained over the years, but if the Bible is not playing an important part in your life today, then you will not be able to effectively encourage others to understand and use it.

I recommend that every leader who has a teaching ministry should be reading the Bible in three different ways:

Devotionally   Every day or as frequently as you can. Reading devotionally means reading in order to hear God speak into your life; reading to receive spiritual nourishment. Whether you use one of the many notes or guides which are available or just read the Bible on its own, this is the foundation of Bible reading.

Thoughtfully   If you are going to teach, you need to prepare. Not simply by reading course notes which may have been prescribed for your group, but by using commentaries and other tools to dig into the Bible passage for yourself. There are a wealth of commentaries at all levels available today and you don't have to be an academic to use them.

Narratively   Read the Bible like you read a novel. Nobody reads the latest bestseller by reading half a page a day. We sit down and read a solid chunk so we can get a grasp of the characters and the plot. We need to do the same with the Bible. Set aside time to read through a gospel, or a letter, or the life of an Old Testament character like Abraham. Haven't got time? It takes only about 20 minutes to read Mark's gospel.

Reflect

Where am I with my own reading of the Bible? How important is it to me?

Preparing to teach   Helping a small group to get into the Bible for themselves is much more difficult than simply talking to them for 20 minutes. There is a danger for most of us that we spend too long telling people things and too little time letting them learn for themselves. I find it really helpful to plan out the framework for a small group teaching session, marking the amount of time I want to spend on each section. Something like this:

7.30   Introductions/anyone new?
7.35   Brainstorm together on theme
7.38   Brief introduction to topic

7.42 First discussion question in pairs
7.48 Write up main points of answers
7.52 Pray over issues raised by discussion
8.00 Whole group discuss second question
8.10 Whole group discuss third question
8.20 Sum up discussion
8.25 Silent reflection as each group member writes down one thing they have learned to take away with them
8.30 Sharing of pastoral needs for prayer
8.35 Prayer

It may look very prescriptive but it is extremely helpful. Firstly, it keeps me under control and brings me back to the point when I'm tempted to ramble. Secondly, it means that discussions don't drag on too long with people talking about all sorts of topics because they've finished what was set. Thirdly, you don't have to stick rigidly to it! Any element can be extended or reduced and the framework will give you an idea what will need to be cut out later (or how much the meeting is going to overrun!).

Reflect

How much thought do I give to the practical mechanics of the way a study works?

Basic tools Alongside your Bible it's helpful to have some basic tools: a concordance, a dictionary and commentaries:

A concordance is basically an index to the Bible. You can't remember where a particular verse comes from? Think of a key word and the concordance will find you the reference. You want to know what the Bible says about 'bread'? Again, the concordance is the place to start. In the days when everyone used the traditional Authorised Version of the Bible, recommending a concordance was easy. Today things are more tricky. My personal recommendation is to buy a Bible which includes a concordance. That way you know it applies to the version of the Bible you're using and when you need to use it in the middle of the group session you've got it to hand.

A Bible dictionary gives the meaning and background to a whole range of Bible topics. It's the place to start if you want to know when Isaiah wrote or where Ur is, or what the Bible says about the Second Coming.

A commentary provides an explanation of the text of the Bible. There are commentaries which cover the whole Bible and those which cover only a book or two. Whole Bible commentaries tend to be a bit frustrating, telling you the things you know and leaving out the things you're really interested in. Over a period of time it's best to build up your own library of commentaries on individual books of the Bible.

Reflect

What books do I already own? What books can I easily borrow? What books ought I to buy? And how am I going to find/make time to read them?

Learning to ask questions Everyone has been to a Bible study group where a question has been asked which is so simple no one is willing to answer. And probably most of us have been in groups where the questions are so vague any answer will do. Asking good questions is not easy.

Try to avoid asking questions which:

- just require a yes or no answer. 'Do you think the people were glad to be fed?'
- just require facts to be quoted from the passage. 'How many people did Jesus feed?'
- are impossible to answer. 'How long did it take to feed all these people?' (We're not told!)
- require specialist knowledge. 'How much fish and bread is required to meet the daily nutritional requirements of an adult?'
- are pointless. Like the one above, for instance.

Try instead to ask questions which seek to interpret or apply the passage. For example:

- to explore how the people reacted to the miracle you could ask: 'What advantages would there be to having a king who could work miracles?'
- to consider our response today ask: 'What might be the modern equivalents of the loaves and fishes?'

This second question is likely to produce fairly simplistic answers – so follow it up with questions about how we give and who we give to and how much it should cost us. In Prime Minister's Question Time, the questioner starts with an innocuous question then follows it up with a supplementary question which is where the real sting is. We don't want to catch people out or trip them up, but we do want to move them on from superficial answers to thinking seriously. So follow up easy opening questions with those that are more searching and detailed. Be ready to pick up on stock answers and clichés and encourage a deeper look.

The purpose of asking questions is not to get answers but to help people think. If you ask good questions there will often be more than one right answer. If that bothers you, think of the way that different preachers will bring out different points from the same passage. But thinking through answers to questions should:

- challenge our assumptions
- make us think in new ways
- encourage us to examine our own attitudes and lifestyle

Reflect

How much thought do I put into the questions I'm going to ask? Do I allow the questions, and the answers, to challenge my own life?

Don't just stick to discussion; there are many different ways of getting into the Bible:

- listen, meditate, reflect in silence, or with background music
- act out or mime the Bible story
- create a poster, painting, model, collage . . . expressing some element of the passage
- role-play the characters in the story
- create an audio or video interpretation, complete with music and sound effects
- use hymns or songs based on biblical passages
- use case studies
- play games

Reflect

How open am I to approaching the Bible other than through the traditional 'read around and discuss' approach?

Ideas

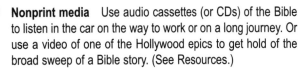

Nonprint media   Use audio cassettes (or CDs) of the Bible to listen in the car on the way to work or on a long journey. Or use a video of one of the Hollywood epics to get hold of the broad sweep of a Bible story. (See Resources.)

Other versions   Try a version of the Bible like **The Message** (see Resources) to give yourself a new insight into familiar passages.

Try re-writing   Take a familiar passage of Scripture and re-write it in language suitable for:

- a five-year-old
- someone who has had no contact with Christianity
- someone who has heard it so many times it no longer has any impact

Explore a story   For example, tackle the story of Esau and Jacob by writing imaginary letters from the different characters to a magazine agony aunt: 'Dear Marje, I sold my birthright for a mess of pottage and I think I've made a bad bargain. What should I do? Yours, Esau.' Write the answers too.

Take a field trip   When you're studying Joseph and Moses, arrange a trip to the British Museum and see some of the incredible artefacts and displays which will open up your understanding of the Bible.

Listen   Invite a storyteller to come and *tell* Bible stories to the group.

GROUP FOCUS

Have one member of the group read Luke 15. Then read the chapter again allocating different people to read the parts of the narrator, Pharisees, Jesus, sheep owner, woman, younger son, father, servant, older brother. Act the three stories without using any words.

Individually write down:

- anything which has struck you from the stories that you never noticed before
- your favourite part of the stories
- the part of the stories that challenges you most

In pairs share what you have written. Then, in groups of four, think about ways the teaching of the passage can be opened up. Each group should devise five questions which could be used to stimulate group discussion. Each group in turn asks their questions to the whole group, who respond briefly to each question. Then together consider:

- which were the most helpful questions?
- why were they helpful?
- what problems about asking questions became apparent?

Pick the five most helpful questions (they needn't all have come from the same group) and discuss them more fully.

Read 2 Timothy 3:14–17. On a large sheet of paper list the purposes of Scripture as given in the passage. Add any other purpose you can think of and find Bible references to support your claim.

For each purpose in turn, try to think of:

- one Bible story which illustrates the purpose
- one daily life situation to which that purpose applies
- a method of tackling the Bible story in order to both understand and to relate it to the life situation

Try out fully, or in part, as many of these methods as you have time for.

Review

What difference did the different ways of reading the Bible passages make to:

- understanding the passage?
- the dynamics of the group?

What methods of getting into the Bible did you find most helpful? Why? Least helpful? Why?

Resources

Some useful videos which should be available from most libraries and video shops:

The Bible: In the Beginning
Gospel According to St Matthew   (Passolini's classic in black and white)
Gospel Road   (Johnny Cash – musical account of the gospel story)
The Greatest Story Ever Told
Jesus
Jesus of Nazareth
Joseph and The Amazing Technicolour Dreamcoat
King David

King of Kings
Miracle Maker
Moses the Lawgiver
The Prince of Egypt
Samson and Delilah
The Ten Commandments
Testament (series of nine Old Testament stories produced by Bible Society and C4 Wales and shown on TV)

And some useful books:

Mind Games Simon Hall. Scripture Union. Background information and over 50 ready-to-use resources to enable groups to meet God through experience and feeling. Includes techniques to explore creativity, ritual and sacrament, meditation and fantasy, role-play etc. Buy a copy and read it, even if the idea frightens you a bit. Not everything in the book is for every group (what book can achieve that!) but it will broaden your horizons.

100 Instant Discussion Starters John Buckeridge. Kingsway. A more conservative approach, but plenty of ideas for getting away from the straightforward question and answer approach to Bible study.

25 Sketches about Proverbs and *50 Sketches about Jesus* David Burt. Kingsway. Two books of material for those who'd like to present Biblical material dramatically.

The Bible Unwrapped David Dewey. Scripture Union. Offers eight different approaches to Bible study.

The Bible with Pleasure Stephen Motyer. Crossway Books. Recognising and enjoying the different types of writing which make up the Bible.

Journey into the Bible John Drane. Scripture Union. Accessible and stimulating introduction to many issues raised by reading the Bible.

Knowing God's Ways J Patton Taylor. Scripture Union. Accessible and readable introduction to the Old Testament.

Be an Expert (in 137 minutes) in Interpreting the Bible Richard Briggs. Scripture Union. Short, entertaining and informative guide to biblical interpretation.

The Bible in Outline John Balchin et al. Scripture Union. Brilliant summaries of all the books of the Bible.

Discovering the New Testament Simon Jones. Crossway Books. An overview of the New Testament in twelve weeks.

Understanding the Bible John Stott. Scripture Union. Classic book on the background to the Bible.

How to Read the Bible for All Its Worth Gordon D Fee & Douglas Stuart. An in-depth look at how to get the best out of the different genres of writing in the Bible.

Build Your Own Bible Study Eric Harmer. Bible Reading Fellowship. A beginner's guide to leading Bible study groups.

Group materials

There are lots of books providing ready-made discussion programmes for Bible teaching in small groups. They do save a lot of time and anguish in preparation. But use them as a starting point only. Add to their ideas techniques you've come across from this book or elsewhere and customise the study to fit your group. For catalogues, write to:

Scripture Union, 207–209 Queensway, Bletchley, Milton Keynes, MK2 2EB. SU supply the Lifebuilder range, which is very popular and includes a vast array of titles. They also publish a wide variety of other small group and study materials. They will also send you free samples of Bible reading notes for your group.

IVP, 38 De Montfort Street, Leicester LE1 7GP. As well as the obvious Bible study courses from IVP, take a look at the Crossway Bible Guides which combine simple commentary with questions for group or personal study.

Christian Focus Publications, Geanies House, Fearn, Tain, Scotland IV20 1TW. A mix of study materials for groups and commentaries for leaders.

Study books/commentaries

As a Bible dictionary/handbook, *The Lion Bible Handbook* is a good, though basic, starting point.

The New Bible Dictionary IVP. In my view this is the most comprehensive Bible dictionary and well worth the high price.

Series of commentaries which will be helpful to small group leaders include:

The Bible Speaks Today IVP. Not verse by verse commentaries, rather the authors write more fully on larger 'chunks'. Good for getting a broad picture and unpacking issues.

Daily Study Bible New Testament William Barclay. St Andrew Press. Fascinating background, comment and application. Also excellent for devotional reading.

Word Bible Commentary Word Publishing. Probably the most accessible of the more scholarly and technical commentaries for leaders who really want to dig deep.

If you're looking for a fresh approach to the Bible, particularly if you aim to sit down and read large sections at one time, you might like to try:

The Message Eugene Peterson. NavPress. Striking, modern American paraphrase.

The Book of God Walter Wangerin. Lion. The Bible written as a novel. He has followed this up with *Paul:* the life of Paul in a similar style.

J B Phillips produced one of the first modern paraphrases of the Bible over fifty years ago. It's readily available second-hand and still an interesting and stimulating read.

Reflect

What have I learned about myself and my Bible reading habits? The way I ask questions? What do I need to do to develop my own understanding and appreciation of the Bible?

Takeaway

How can I vary the way the Bible is read/presented in my small group? How can I encourage members of my group to get to grips with the Bible for themselves? How can I introduce my group members to the vast array of resources which could help them interact with the Bible?

Diary

Week 1 – Read a big chunk of the Bible in one go? Impossible! I have enough trouble with half a dozen verses in my Bible reading notes.

Week 2 – Watched Prince of Egypt and kept thinking 'Is that bit in the Bible or did they make it up?' Decided to check it out. Started at Genesis 37 and got hooked. Next thing I knew I'd finished it. Fourteen chapters!

Week 3 – Not quite so easy in Hebrews . . . !

4 The Bible into Life

Applying the Bible to issues of the everyday

What does the Bible say about . . . homosexuality, for instance? Or cloning? Euthanasia? Divorce? Conservation? Third World debt? What about cosmetic surgery? Or test tube babies? Consumerism? Or global warming? Just where would you start to look in the Bible for answers?

It's not just a matter of looking up a verse or two which can be trotted out to prove a point. The best theological minds of centuries have wrestled with some of these issues – while some of the topics are so new and so complex that the study's hardly begun. Even where study's been done, there is disagreement. Yet Christians have a responsibility to try to understand the broad sweep of the Bible's teaching on these areas of debate, to try to see how they fit into the teaching on other related subjects.

While there is a danger that we teach the Bible in such a *spiritual* way that it never has any bearing on everyday life, there is also a danger that in seeking to apply the Bible to current, practical issues we simply teach our own opinions, fears and prejudices.

If our limited view of the Bible is a problem, then so is our limited view of the world. Most of us are not experts on international politics or medical ethics or any of the many topics which challenge our faith and understanding. So applying the Bible to everyday life, although an essential part of Christian discipleship, is something we should undertake with a strong spirit of humility. That doesn't mean that we shouldn't hold definite views on topical issues – but we should always be ready to listen to other opinions, particularly those held by other Bible-believing Christians, and be ready to accept that we may be wrong in part, or entirely.

Reflect

How open am I to really finding out what the Bible has to say on a topic? How easily do I adopt views which I have never really thought through?

Pastoral Sensitivity   Even where there is no disagreement within the group about a particular issue, many topics will hold *different emotional weights* for different people in the group. For example, all the group may agree that sex outside marriage is wrong. But:

- a young person struggling to remain chaste
- an unmarried parent
- a parent whose children are promiscuous or living with someone
- a happily married person
- someone aged 99

will react to that truth in different ways and need different levels and types of support in working through the implications of that truth in their lives. Most of us are tolerant of the faults in others that exist in us – but intolerant of others who struggle with issues we do not find a problem.

Reflect

How aware am I of the different situations of members of the group and how they are likely to be affected by different topics?

Good habits   If we're going to see what the Bible has to say on current issues there are a number of things we need to do.

Read the Bible   Get into the habit of reading the Bible so as to see the broad picture. For example, if you want to know what the Bible teaches about marriage, you could start with a concordance and look up all the references to marriage and make notes on the specific points which come up. Then read through the stories of some of the people of the Bible and reflect on how their marriages worked. What other issues come up? What about singleness, divorce, adultery, children, widowhood? And other related topics?

Read, listen, watch   Read newspapers and magazines, watch television, listen to the radio and think critically (ie try and understand and evaluate – not judge negatively) about the way marriage and personal relationships are presented.

Relate   Try and relate the Bible to the culture. Where are they at odds? Where do they agree? What does modern society need to hear from the Bible? What do Christians need to learn from society?

Think   Put yourself in the shoes of real people. This is essential. So much teaching about how Christians should live simply reflects the things we personally feel OK about and doesn't try to take into account the pressures other people face. For example, if you come to the conclusion that a divorced Christian should not re-marry, then put yourself in the position of a woman with young children whose husband has abandoned her and who longs for warmth and companionship and a father for her kids. If you come to the conclusion that divorce is always wrong for Christians, put yourself in the position of someone whose partner is an alcoholic, or violent, or abusive. You may be driven back to the Bible to re-examine your conclusions. But even if you keep the same conclusions, you will be more understanding of the difficulties others face and less likely to be glibly judgemental.

There are plenty of Christian books on topical issues but it's best to struggle with Scripture and culture (Bible and TV!)

on your own first and seek to come to at least tentative conclusions before absorbing other people's conclusions.

Check policy Check with your church leaders what your church's policy is on different issues. If in your small group you are teaching that re-marriage after divorce is wrong yet your church re-marries divorcees then the church is giving out mixed messages. Talk with your minister or leaders about the issue and try to understand her/his point of view where it differs from yours. It's OK to have different views on these issues, but as a leader you are someone under authority (see page 7) and you need to agree a policy about what you teach.

Be self aware Try and be aware of your own sensitivities, vulnerabilities and biases. Some years ago when I was about to be involved in counselling people about sexual problems in marriage I went on a training course. The first part of it was not about other people's problems, it was about coming to terms with me! What embarrassed me? What hurt me? What shocked me? There are some topics we should not attempt to teach because, although we may have an intellectual understanding of them, we have not come to terms with them emotionally and spiritually.

Reflect

How much time can I give to making myself aware of the important issues in society today?

Ideas

Watch soaps Watch *EastEnders*, *Brookside* or *Coronation Street* with a pen and paper at hand. Note down issues which are portrayed. What *answers* does the soap offer? Use all or some of these as topics for study. Try the same exercise with daily newspapers or popular magazines.

Ask people Like the local political parties, conduct a mini survey in the streets around where your group meets. Ask people to identify the issues they think are most significant. You might also ask if they think the church or the Bible has anything to say on these issues? Use the results to identify areas for study. They could also be useful in evangelism (see chapter 10).

Share testimonies Have a group testimony evening. Ask people to share, not about how they came to faith, but about how the Bible has shaped and influenced their lives since.

Invite a speaker Invite a local Christian MP, businessperson, teacher, doctor etc, to talk to the group about how they try to apply the teaching of the Bible to their work.

Get involved Look for a local issue where you can get practically involved. Spend time as a group working out what the Bible has to say about the issue, then get stuck in. Periodically stop to reflect on how well theory and practice match. It's easy to say, 'This is what we should do' from the comfort of our armchairs. But when we are personally involved we often have to re-think our assumptions.

GROUP FOCUS

Choose an issue which is topical in the news or in church life. Divide into three groups.

Group 1: Look up in the Bible all passages giving direct teaching about this issue. Write references on a large sheet of paper and summarise teaching.

Group 2: Brainstorm the stories in the Bible relating to the issue. What application might we make of these stories to contemporary life? List stories and applications on a large sheet of paper.

Group 3: Brainstorm all the topics relating to the one which has been chosen and list them. Look up Bible passages for as many as possible. On large sheet of paper summarise your findings.

Example: If you choose the issue of war (perhaps because there is a debate about whether the country should be involved in a particular conflict) then **Group 1** would look at passages which teach directly about war; **Group 2** would look at stories in which God's people fought wars; **Group 3** might come up with related issues like peacemaking, forgiveness etc.

Lay the three sheets of conclusions alongside each other on the floor. Share out among the group a selection of newspapers. Each person should go through the paper tearing out articles which relate to the topic. Arrange these around your findings, drawing lines from the articles to the parts of your findings which seem to relate. Where nothing relates discuss together what should be added.

When you have done this, review. Try and agree together either some basic principles which have emerged (eg war is justified if . . .) or some areas which need further investigation (eg does the Bible say anything about the use of nuclear weapons?).

The next stage is to see how these findings affect everyday life. Brainstorm a list of the sort of people who are likely to be directly affected. For the subject of war, these might include politicians, people in armed forces, aid agencies and missionary organisations working in affected countries. Split into twos or threes, each taking one of these categories. Imagine that someone in your category has written asking for advice on how to live as a Christian in their situation and compose a letter in reply. For example, in a letter to a Christian MP you would seek to spell out the principles about when war is or isn't justified and how she/he should come to conclusions about how to vote on the issue. Don't try to tell people what to do; guide them through the process of how to come to their own conclusions.

Identify people within your own congregation or known to you who would be practically involved in this issue and pray for them. Take up Paul's injunction in 1 Timothy 2:1,2 and pray for government, local authorities, media etc.

Finally, it's necessary to look at how the issue affects each of us personally. What challenges face us as Christians regarding this issue. Does it have relevance to our jobs, our family, our personal or social life or our church life? It may seem that no one in the group is directly affected. But what responsibilities do we have? Should we, for instance, (sticking to our war example):

- lobby the government?
- support relief agencies?
- make links with armed services personnel?
- preach sermons on the topic?
- write to the press?

Brainstorm ideas for involvement and list them. Then spend time in prayer, seriously asking God to show you what, if anything, he wants you to do. After prayer, look at the list again and decide how the group can take this issue forward practically. Don't forget to discuss with your church leaders before taking action!

Review

Make lists of the benefits and the problems in trying to apply faith practically. Give opportunity for the group to share any parts of the study where they felt threatened, challenged or bored. Try and agree guidelines for groups in the church who want to explore the practical application of their faith.

Resources

The **Connect Bible Studies** published by Scripture Union (or available as a download from www.connectbiblestudies.com) explore key issues raised by contemporary films, TV programmes, books and music. Titles available are: **Harry Potter; The Matrix; All that you can't leave behind/U2; Billy Elliot; Chocolat; TV Game Shows; How to be Good; Destiny's Child: 'Survivor'; AI: Artificial Intelligence; Lord of the Rings; The Simpsons; Iris; Dido: No Angel; Sven: On Football; Superheroes; The Pullman Trilogy** – with others being added all the time.

Christian Life and Today's World   London Bible College & Scripture Union – a book and video package taking up the challenge of living as Christians in a postmodern society.
The Contemporary Christian   John Stott. IVP. A plea to the church to listen to God's Word and God's world.
The Moral Maze   David Cook. SPCK. Not easy reading but a fascinating look at the way Christians can use the Bible as a guide to ethical problems.
Churchgoing and Christian Ethics   Robin Gill. Cambridge University Press. Examines surveys showing how church communities view moral issues.

To think about . . .

'One of our greatest needs in today's church is a sensitive awareness of the world around us. If we are true servants of Jesus Christ, we will keep our eyes open (as he did) to human need, and our ears cocked to pick up cries of anguish. And we will respond compassionately and constructively (as again he did) to people's pain.' **The Contemporary Christian** John Stott. IVP.

Reflect

How comfortable am I in discussing contemporary issues in my small group? How sensitive am I to the pain that some issues will bring to others in the group? How willing am I to put aside my dogmatic opinions and come to Scripture ready to learn?

Takeaway

What issues would be particularly relevant to my group at this time? How would my group respond to an approach like the Connect Bible Studies? Would they find it difficult to watch a secular video in a Christian housegroup? Is the approach we used as leaders in the **Group Focus** for unpacking issues suitable for my small group or would it make too many demands on them?

Diary

Week 1 – Determined not to compromise with the world. Our group is going to be firmly based on Scripture. We're not going to chase after contemporary issues. I thought Daniel would be a safe bet, but somehow we got into a discussion about politics and how Christians should relate to a government with non-Christian values. Not what I was looking for!

Week 2 – Tried a New Testament study this week but the life of Paul led us into pluralism, materialism and racism.

Week 3 – I think I'm getting the message. If we come honestly to the Bible, the Holy Spirit will help us apply it to the world we live in. Can't bring myself to start with the world ('Today we'll talk about sex!') But we're going to tackle the Sermon on the Mount next. There can't be many issues we won't come across there!

5 Praying in Small Groups

Problems, pitfalls and fresh ideas to resolve them

Why pray in small groups? Well, apart from all the general reasons for praying, I'd like to recommend four good reasons for making prayer part of a small group programme.

Firstly, small groups are a safe place to learn how to pray. Not just new Christians but many who have been Christians for some time find prayer in public very intimidating. In a friendly and supportive small group there's opportunity for the shyest and most timid to learn. Secondly, small groups are good places for people to learn how to pray in different ways. It's easy to get stale in our prayer life and different techniques and ideas for prayer can be safely explored in a small group. Thirdly, prayer is a great way for people to support and encourage one another. An effective small group allows people to open up about their needs and difficulties – and their joys. And fourthly, bearing in mind that home groups tend to be introverted, prayer can help the group look outward into their community and the wider world.

Reflect

What do you find difficult about praying with others? What makes it easier? Are you looking forward to the experience of praying with this group?

What to pray about?   Anything and everything! For a start there's:

- needs of individual group members
- ministry and witness of group members; in the same way that we pray for missionaries overseas, we can also pray for the mission field each of us has among families, friends, neighbours, work colleagues etc
- people who've stopped coming to the group
- people you're trying to encourage to come along to the group
- local neighbourhood
- work of the church and denomination to which you belong
- issues that arise from Bible study and discussion together
- plus a whole range of local, national and international topics

And don't forget other types of prayer – thanksgiving, confession, reflection, meditation.

Reflect

What is the range of your prayer life? Do you pray over the same few topics or are you inspired by the things you see and hear and read to pray widely?

Pray for your group   Draw up a list of the people in your group (or likely to be if you are starting a new group). Write down what you know of their interests and work (paid and unpaid). Start praying for them now, yourself.

Effective prayer   How can we make prayer enjoyable and effective?

- Keep it **brief**. It's usually better to pray in short sections rather than for an extended period.
- Keep it **real**. Focus on issues which are of real concern to the group. Pray specifically, not just 'God bless so and so'.
- Keep it **confidential**. Don't discuss outside of the group anything group members share for prayer, or say in prayer.
- Make it **practical**. Be aware that God may want to use *us* to answer prayers. So be alert for opportunities to be practically involved in the issues you pray about.
- Make it **continuous**. Encourage group members not only to pray at the meetings but to commit themselves to pray about key issues at other times.
- Take time to **report answers** to prayer and thank God for them.

Problems and pitfalls   People don't always naturally want to pray! Use some prayer ideas which involve reading or writing prayers as a way of encouraging those reluctant to pray spontaneously. Never put pressure on people to pray or suggest that they are less spiritual than those who can 'ramble on' for hours in prayer.

Sometimes praying gets stale. Variety is one solution. Pick issues for prayer that really fire people's imagination and interest. Don't be afraid to spend time learning about or discussing an issue before praying about it. The learning and discussion is all part of the prayer process.

What's wrong with just praying in the 'old-fashioned' way? Nothing at all! But for many of us it easily becomes routine and dull. New ways of praying don't give our prayers any greater value with God – but they do stimulate our thoughts to pray more intelligently. For example, a prayer walk around the local community isn't any more effective than sitting in a room and praying for the community. But the stimulus of being outside may well suggest to you all sorts of topics for prayer that you would never think of indoors.

Ideas

Newspapers   Divide a newspaper up between members of the group. Everyone should choose one item from their page to pray about. For example, if you want to pray about a specific issue then give out the relevant pages from a variety of newspapers to provide fuel and inspiration for prayer. If you want to pray for children and young people spend time looking at the magazines and comics they read.

Write a psalm This is a great way of really getting into praise and thanksgiving. The psalms often work by patterns of repetition. For example, 'I will extol the Lord at all times', the first line of Psalm 34, is repeated in different words in the second line: 'His praise will always be on my lips'. This is a fairly easy pattern for individuals or pairs to reproduce. Alternatively, you can go round the group, each person adding an extra line.

Pray in pairs When the whole group is praying together it's often hard for the less extrovert to pray aloud. They're afraid of starting to pray at the same time as someone else or just nervous about praying with everyone listening. Praying in pairs gives everyone an opportunity. Pairs simply need to agree who prays first and then 'go for it'. When one of the pair finishes praying the other starts. All the pairs (and the trio – there's always an odd number when you decide to do this!) pray at once. Be careful not to put pressure on people. Anyone should be able to pray silently (in or out of a pair) if they prefer.

Pray silently for the people on either side Ask people to be quiet and think about the person sitting on either side of them, and then pray for them. (If this is a new group spend a few minutes first allowing people to introduce themselves.)

Prayer requests on cards Give each member of the group a small card and ask them to write one prayer request on it. Shuffle the cards and give them out. Each person prays (aloud or silently) for the request on the card they receive. Another way of using request cards is to have a box near the door into which members can drop prayer requests they bring with them. This idea can be extended out into the community (see chapter 10 on outreach).

Prayer diaries and journals Ask each member to keep a diary of their prayer life in between meetings. They should note the things they pray for and any ways in which God answered their prayers. You can keep a group diary in the same way.

Response prayers Choose a simple response like 'We thank you, Lord' or 'Lord, we are sorry'. Group members briefly mention a subject and the group responds. For example:

'For your creation' – 'We thank you, Lord'
'For our selfishness' – 'Lord, we are sorry'

Only use one response at a time or you'll end up being sorry for blessings and thankful for sins!

Name only prayers Pray for people in need simply by mentioning their first name and then having a period of silence.

Another way of doing this is to have some small candles (and something to stand them on – a tray of sand is ideal). Members of the group take a candle, light it and say the name of the person they are praying for. The group pray silently until the next person takes a candle.

Silence Don't be afraid of silent prayer. Do give some guidance as to how people can use the silence. A visual focus is helpful. This could be as simple as a list of prayer requests. Or ask someone to create a focus – flower arrangement, photos, arrangement of objects, simple sculpture – to stimulate prayer. Or ask each member of the group to bring one object which will serve as a prayer reminder and place these on a table in the centre of the group. Remind them that it's OK to pray with eyes open!

Prayer board Have a flip chart or large sheet of paper available and, with suitable music playing, encourage group members to come and write prayer requests on it. These can be personal, for other people, or for national or international issues. Allow plenty of time for this process, giving people space for reflection. When everyone has finished writing, ask them to gather round the board and read the requests before the leader prays for the topics, or members pray for the topics out loud, or members pray for the topics silently.

Written prayers Encourage people to bring prayers chosen from the many published books of prayer which are available, or to write their own prayers and bring them to the group. Or spend time in the group, singly or in pairs or threes writing prayers which are then read. Don't forget that hymns and songs can be used as prayers and that there are many prayers in the Bible.

Music Choose music to provide a focus and stimulus for prayer. Worship music (of whatever style) can be a focus for praise, adoration or meditation. Something from the pop charts (listen to it first – you may be surprised at some of the content!) could be used to stimulate prayer for the world we live in.

Pray through the Bible Read a short passage from the Bible together and simply pray for the issues which it raises.

Prayer walks The idea of a prayer walk is to walk the streets of an area in small groups praying (aloud or silently) as you walk. It's not as terrifying as it seems (as long as you don't keep your eyes closed while you pray!). It works very well in alerting the group to a whole range of needs and situations in the area. Why not start by prayer walking your own church building? Go into each room and pray for the activities which take place there. Pray at the doors for the people who come in each week. Stand outside and pray for the community surrounding the building.

Positions Experiment using different positions for prayer: standing, kneeling, sitting, even lying flat on the floor.

Evangelistic prayer Each member of the group identifies two people (friends, family, colleagues, neighbours) they would like to see come to faith. These are shared in a pair or a three, agreeing not only to pray for them at meetings but on a regular basis. Don't forget to report back to the group any encouragements in your witness.

Ephesians 3:14–21 Pray this prayer replacing the word 'you' with 'us' or with the names of specific individuals or another group. There are other Biblical prayers which can be simply adapted for modern use. For example, use Solomon's prayer (1 Kings 3:9) for situations where wisdom is needed or someone takes on new responsibility; Elisha's prayer (2 Kings 6:17) where someone is fearful and lacking assurance; the prayer of Jabez (1 Chronicles 4:10) in situations where faith to move forward is required; or Nehemiah's prayer (Nehemiah 1:5–11) to pray for the state of the nation or for success in some undertaking.

Praying in tongues Some people may wish to pray in tongues. Make sure all the group understand this and if necessary explain to new members. Make sure everyone knows what the ground rules are regarding interpretation and any other issues.

Mission Most mission societies produce prayer guides, cassettes, videos etc. Make a link with one or two which the group can 'adopt' and pray for regularly. If you have personal links with missionaries, see whether you can use email for up-to-the-minute prayer requests. Invite people into the group to talk about their work. This could be someone from an outside organisation (eg mission society) but could equally be someone from within the church. Some examples could be:

- **a church leader** We expect leaders to pray for others. It can be really helpful to have a leader share honestly and openly her/his prayer needs.
- **someone involved in an area of church life** This could be someone from the parent and toddler group, youth work, senior citizens' group, soup run.
- **someone involved in the practical life of the church** The church caretaker, or someone who organises catering for church events, for example.
- **someone from another small group** Why not invite people from the other small groups, one at a time over several weeks, to share news of their group for prayer?
- **someone from another church or denomination**

GROUP FOCUS

Read aloud* all or part of various psalms of praise. You could use parts of Psalms 96, 97, 100, 104, 136, for example, finishing with Psalm 150. Attempt to create your own psalm of praise in the style of Psalm 150, each member of the group contributing one line, with someone writing it down as you create it. When complete, read it aloud together.

In pairs share with your partner: 'If I could change one thing . . .'

- **in the world** it would be . . .
- **in the church** it would be . . .
- **in my life** it would be . . .

Pray together, picking up the points mentioned.

Together as a group read* Matthew 6:5–18. Discuss: What is Jesus opposing? What is Jesus encouraging?

Divide the Lord's Prayer into sections and give each section a title. Write the titles on a large sheet of paper leaving gaps under each. Under each title list current prayer topics which would fit into that section.

Reflect

How does our individual/small group/church life reflect the balance shown by the Lord's Prayer? For example, do we major on petitionary prayer (asking for things) to the exclusion of other types of prayer? Sing, or listen to a recording of, a version of the Lord's Prayer; then pray silently.

Read* in pairs one of Paul's prayers. Here's a list:

Romans 1:7–10; 15:5,6; 15:13
1 Corinthians 1:3–9
2 Corinthians 1:2–4; 13:7–10
Galatians 1:3–5
Ephesians 1:15–23; 3:14–21
Philippians 1:2–6; 1:9–11
Colossians 1:2–4; 1:9–12
1 Thessalonians 1:2–4; 3:10–13
2 Thessalonians 1:2,3; 1:11,12; 2:13–17

Each pair reads a different prayer. List the main points. Together, compile a combined list of topics from Paul's prayers. Using one or more of the methods listed under prayer ideas, pray through some of the topics.

Brainstorm any more ideas for ways to pray which haven't already been covered in this session.

***Reading aloud** Don't ask the whole group to read round a passage unless you are sure that no one will be embarrassed by reading aloud. Similarly, do not ask any individual to read aloud unless you are sure they are happy to do so.

Review

What have you found most helpful in this session? What have you found unhelpful? Choose an appropriate method of prayer to end the group.

To think about . . .

'Prayers that have much life and affection in them are in a special manner pleasing to God.' Matthew Henry

Resources

Praying Together Allan Harkness. Scripture Union. A slim booklet which tackles difficulties and makes constructive suggestions to improve group prayer.

Multi-sensory Prayer Sue Wallace. Scripture Union. Over 60 innovative ideas for meeting God in prayer. Intended for young people but also suitable for adult groups willing to be innovative.

Dangerous Praying David Spriggs. Scripture Union. Inspirational ideas for individuals and groups.

Serious Prayer Trev Gregory. Scripture Union. Book and video to help youth leaders communicate the importance of prayer to their groups.

Operation World OM Publishing. Also available on a CD rom. Comprehensive guide to praying for world mission.

Praying the Jesus Prayer Brother Ramon and Simon Barrington-Ward. Bible Reading Fellowship. Outlines an ancient yet simple form of contemplative prayer, rooted in Scripture.

The Lion Prayer Collection Mary Batchelor. Lion. A very comprehensive book of prayers from all ages and tradi-

tions. But there are huge numbers of books of prayers (new and secondhand), so take time to browse.

See also the resources listed in the next chapter which concentrates on worship.

Reflect

What have I learned? What practical step can I take to deepen my own prayer life? How can I best help to develop the prayer life of the group? Who am I praying for? Who is praying for me?

Takeaway

What methods of prayer will be most helpful for my group? What topics for prayer could be used to broaden our prayer life?

Diary

Week 1 – First session on the subject of prayer. Gave them comprehensive Bible study on importance of always praying. No time left at end to pray.

Week 2 – Decided to get on with prayer right from start so cut out singing, talking and coffee. They have a long way to go! It was very difficult to keep them praying for an hour and half – they kept lapsing into silence and I had to encourage them along.

Week 3 – Kingston came in really upset. He's been having a lot of problems at work. After we'd listened to him for a while, someone said 'Why don't we pray?'. So we did, with everyone contributing. Later, as we were having coffee, we got into a discussion about work and decided we could all do with some prayer. We got together in pairs and prayed for one another. They want to make it a regular feature of the group.

---

6 Worshipping in Small Groups

So much more than singing

I heard of a man who was asked to lead a small midweek group in his home. He was very enthusiastic about it. When the group arrived they found he had moved all the furniture out of the room and set out in rows some wooden chairs with a hymnbook on every one, together with a lectern and a small keyboard at the front – all transported from the church!

We don't all do it so obviously – but there is a great temptation to try and make small groups a miniature version of Sunday meetings. And this is especially so when it comes to worship.

When someone announces, 'And now we're going to have a time of worship' what do you expect? Singing! Singing is great! I love it. Old hymns and modern songs – even some pretty corny choruses. But singing has hijacked worship. Worship is so much more than simply singing. This is a particular problem for small groups because unless, among your eight or ten people, you just happen to have a talented musician or singer, worship in a small group can be pretty dire. Various publishers have produced cassettes, CDs and books to enable small groups without musicians to be able to sing, and they can be useful. But before we even think about singing we need to consider some other aspects of worship.

Prayer, of course, is an essential component of worship. We have already considered creative forms of prayer and although there may be some overlap, for this chapter we shall concentrate on other elements of worship.

Reflect

What experiences do I have of worship other than what happens in church on a Sunday?

Using the Bible In the **Ideas** section you'll find some creative ways of using the Bible to worship and in the **GROUP FOCUS** section we'll study some of the passages which teach about worship. The Bible is a neglected book as far as worship is concerned, particularly among evangelicals. We are so focussed on study that we usually only use the Bible to read the passage for study. But the Bible is full of words of praise, adoration, confession and petition that we can take and make our own. We use a hymn book because most of us would find it very difficult to compose an original hymn or song on the spot. Many of us struggle to express ourselves in any form at all. We want to tell God how great he is. We want to say we love him. We want, at times, to say sorry because we've failed him. But it can sound so trite in our own everyday words. Get in the habit of using the words of the Bible to express the things you can't say well yourself. For example:

Praise: 1 Chronicles 16:8–13; Luke 1:46–55; Revelation 19:6–8.
Confession: Psalm 32, Psalm 51.

Use the 'helpful verses' section that many Bibles have to find others. One of the advantages of using Scripture in this way is that the passages are not neat and well defined but will take our praise, prayer, confession in directions we would otherwise not think of going. Look at Deuteronomy 33:27. The first part of the verse is well known but explore the context. How much of the verses around could you make your own – and in what situations?

Using other resources:

Books Just as there are books of hymns, so there are books of meditations, readings, prayers etc. Don't be afraid to use them and to make them available for other people in the group to use.

Cassettes and CDs Not just to sing along to, but as background music for reflection, to focus on a particular song or piece of music, or spoken word recordings including recordings of Scripture.

Candles Can be a focus for meditation or used symbolically in prayer.

Artefacts A cross, crucifix, icon, picture, flowers, any sort of artistic creation can be used as a worship focus.

Silence Worship doesn't have to be spoken aloud. Time to think, to worship in the heart and mind, can be valuable and powerful. Background music – to blank out other noises and visual distractions – can be helpful.

Movement Get out of your seats. Stand, kneel. Move into other rooms, the garden or the street. Dance if there's room!

Reflect

What excites me about using new forms of worship? What puts me off? How important is worship to me? How much am I prepared to risk to improve it?

Celebration of Discipline One of the most stimulating home group experiences I ever had was in a group where we worked our way through Richard Foster's book *Celebration of Discipline*. The twelve chapters are divided into three groups – 'Inward Disciplines' of meditation, prayer, fasting, study; 'Outward Disciplines' of simplicity, solitude, submission, service; 'Corporate Disciplines' of confession, worship, guidance, celebration. Richard Foster offers simple, practical guidance which will enable any group to try these disciplines, many of which may be new to most. The beauty of it is that you can start small. There is no pressure to become super-spiritual overnight. I well remember the fun (yes, really!) and the challenge of our first tentative steps at fasting and the difference it made to our prayer life. I strongly recommend trying out some or all of these disciplines in your small group.

Ideas

Instead of always having members of the group read from the Bible, listen while it is read on a cassette or CD, or watch a video like the Visual Bible in which the soundtrack is taken directly from Scripture.

If the group is new to the idea of using silence keep the period of silence short to begin with. A minute can seem like eternity. Increase the time as the group becomes more comfortable with it.

Give people ideas about how to use silence, such as:

- focussing on a Bible verse.
- thinking about people who helped lead you to Christ and thanking God for them.
- praying silently for the people on either side of you.
- reading or telling a Bible story allowing silences after each line or so for the group to visualise the story in their minds.
- encouraging the group to listen to what God has to say to them, for example on an issue relating to the study which has been done together. Don't put any pressure on people or make people feel second-rate if they don't 'hear' anything. After the silence ask people to share their thoughts. Unless you are already well established in the area of spiritual gifts, don't be too quick to put labels like 'prophecy', or 'word of knowledge' on what people say. But slowly and carefully learn together to discern the ways in which God speaks through individuals.

Just for fun have a silent coffee break. How can you serve each other with coffee without speaking? Afterwards talk about how we communicate. What are the benefits and the problems of words?

Other worship ideas:

The natural world   Create an Easter garden, on a tray, or in a bottle, and use it as a focus to worship – not only at Easter! Other ideas for a visual focus can be flower arrangements, posters, photos, food, stones, in fact anything. Think about ways of stimulating the sense of touch and smell as well as simply providing a visual focus.

People's gifts   Check out the practical gifts available in your group. Make use of artistic and creative gifts to create visual focus.

Writing   Worship by writing rather than speaking. With some music playing, encourage people to come to a large sheet of paper and write prayer requests/thanksgivings/words of praise and adoration.

Psalms   Choose a psalm of praise (any from 145 to 150 would be suitable). Try different ways of reading it together:

- Divide the group in two and read either alternate verses or alternate halves of each verse.
- Read the whole psalm aloud together, starting quietly and getting louder up to a triumphant conclusion.
- One person reads the first verse, a second person joins for the second verse, third for third, etc. If you have a short psalm and large group, add two people for each verse.

If you have a talented musician then singing is no problem. If not, it's probably best not to use a less than confident musician. Try singing unaccompanied, or sing along to cassettes or CDs.

Don't be afraid to use books:

Books of prayer may help shyer members pray aloud. I remember a man in his seventies who really struggled with the fact that other people in the group could pray aloud and he didn't feel able. One week he came with a little book of prayers tucked into his pocket and during the prayer time read a prayer. It had a powerful effect on the whole group. Written prayers also help us break out of the narrow confines of our usual prayer topics.

Books of poetry and meditations (including hymn books)

Books from the past   C S Lewis points out that old books correct 'the characteristic mistakes of our own period.' (*On Reading Old Books. C S Lewis Essay Collection.* Harper Collins.) They can also bring a radically different way of looking at things. Try for example the *Book of Common Prayer* (especially if you're not from an Anglican tradition) and writers like Augustine, John of the Cross, Matthew Henry, William Law, J C Ryle, C H Spurgeon, G K Chesterton.

Modern writers   Encourage members who read something particularly thought-provoking (whether or not it is from a Christian author) to bring it along to include in worship.

GROUP FOCUS

Go round the group and share your best/worst experience of worship. List the factors that made the experience good/bad. What are the key factors which promote good worship? Which ones can be incorporated into the small group meeting?

For one minute think silently about the good things which have happened in the past week. Each person should write one of these on a sheet of paper. Each person passes their sheet of paper onto the next person, who adds another. When the papers have moved all round the group and everyone has their original sheet back, have a time of rapid thanksgiving prayer for the things listed.

Read 1 Corinthians 14:26–40. The Corinthians came ready to participate. Ask each member to score themselves from 1 to 10 for each of these statements:

- I think and pray about the group before I come.
- I often only realise the group is on at the last minute.
- I love praying aloud.
- I love discussing the Bible.
- I'd rather sit quietly and say nothing.

If your group is full of confident extroverts, then go round and ask everyone to share a Bible verse, a song (they can say it, they don't have to sing it!) poem, thought, challenge, testimony etc. If the group is shyer, then ask the question, 'If we were all about to share something, like the church at Corinth, what sort of thing would you share?' Tease the answers out and then reflect that you have in fact been sharing!

Divide into three groups:

- **Group 1** should look at verses 26–28 and come up with practical guidelines to ensure that everything done in the group meetings should build the group.
- **Group 2** looks at verses 29–33 to draw up practical guidelines by which the group can test what is said and done.
- **Group 3** looks at verses 33–38 and grapples with the question 'Is participation for everyone or just for some?'

Share the answers and set up guidelines for worship and participation within the group. Take time to worship by singing in any of the ways already suggested.

Put a branch with several stems into a pot and place in the centre of the group. Give everyone several labels with string. Each person should write on the label some characteristic of God which is worthy of praise, for example: 'faithful', 'loving', 'strong'. When everyone has written as many as they want, go round the group reading them out. Use a formula like 'Lord I praise and worship you because you are _____' with the rest of the group responding with 'Hallelujah, Amen!' Tie the labels onto the branch. Spend a short time in silence reflecting on the many facets of God's character.

Review

Which parts of the group time worked really well? Which parts did not work well? Could these be changed to work better or are they unsuitable for this group? Does singing enhance worship in a small group? What is the most practical method to encourage good singing?

To think about . . .

'For committed Christians it is impossible to look at Scripture or a sunrise and not worship God from the depth of the soul. It is impossible to ponder God's holiness without a sense of wonder and awe.' *The 77 Habits of Highly Ineffective Christians* Chris Fabry. Crossway Books.

Resources

The Prayers of the New Testament Donald Coggan. Hodder and Stoughton. 1967. Look out for secondhand copies of this book. It's great for your own devotional reading, but it's also a complete collection of every prayer in the New Testament, many of which you can use or adapt for worship.

50 Worship Ideas for Small Groups Stuart Townend. Kingsway. Scriptures, prayers, ideas and song suggestions. Part of a set of materials which includes songsheets and CDs.

50 Creative Worship Ideas Nancy Goudie. Kingsway. Explores ways of using all the senses in worship. A fascinating and creative book.

Multi-sensory Church Sue Wallace. Scripture Union.

Celebration of Discipline Richard Foster. Hodder and Stoughton. See comments above.

How Can I Hear God? Gillian Peall. Scripture Union. Useful reading for groups who want to learn to hear from God in worship, study and prayer.

The Reflective Life Ken Gire. Kingsway. How to pause, reflect and listen to God.

An Anthology for the Church Year H J Richards. Kevin Mayhew Publishers. Anthology of readings, prayers, scriptural texts, poems and meditations.

Flowing Stream/Liturgy of Life/Seasons and Celebrations/The Word in the World/No Empty Phrases Donald Hilton. NCEC. Five anthologies of readings, prayers, meditations and poems.

Lion Christian Poetry Collection/Lion Christian Meditation Collection/Lion Christian Quotation Collection Substantial collections of resources from Lion Publishing.

The Story of Christian Spirituality Gordon Mursell, Ed. Lion Publishing and *Brief History of Christian Music* Lion Publishing – two books which give a historical background to worship which help leaders put contemporary trends into perspective.

Kevin Mayhew Publishers offer a range of resources under the title *The Resource for Small Group Worship.* This includes a leader's manual and five volumes of music books, each of which includes a CD of backing tracks. For the more traditionally minded, they offer a set of 10 CDs providing organ or piano accompaniment to around 200 traditional and modern hymns.

The Visual Bible A series of videos covering Matthew's Gospel and Acts. The narration uses the actual biblical text while the dramatisation, costume, settings etc are as authentic as possible. *The New Media Bible* is similar and covers Genesis and Luke.

There are a great many versions of the Bible available on cassette and any Christian bookshop (or shops like Waterstones and W H Smith) should be able to offer a selection. Various Bible translations are used; some versions having music and sound effects and some just straight reading. As an example,

Hodder and Stoughton publish the Old Testament (abridged) in 20 cassettes and the complete New Testament in 16 cassettes. The NIV translation is used and read by a series of well-known British actors.

Reflect

How committed am I to see the group develop innovative ways of worshipping together? How open am I to the Holy Spirit (through me or others) leading the group in ways I haven't planned?

Takeaway

What objections/fears/worries will my group members have concerning worship? How can I introduce new ideas in a sensitive way? Which ideas for worship should I try out in my group?

Diary

Week 1 – Took my guitar to housegroup. I can pretty much play six songs now. Group were hopeless. Couldn't keep in time with me and kept suggesting songs I can't play.

Week 2 – String snapped while practising so had to go without guitar. Sang all those songs they wanted last week. Everyone surprised that it doesn't sound too bad – in tune most of the time – even without my playing.

Week 3 – Some songs I played (it really helps my playing to have to do it while people are actually singing) and some I didn't. Everyone very encouraging . . . though I don't quite know what Bill means by saying that now we've mastered making a joyful noise we need to learn something about being silent.

---

7 Fellowship

Relationship-building activities to enrich belonging

Why do some small groups seem to have a real 'buzz' about them? The members are always doing something together. They really seem to enjoy each other's company. Other groups find it hard to be sociable during the hour or so they meet and certainly don't want to have anything to do with each other outside the meetings. What makes the difference? In chapter 2 we looked at ways to establish a group and build those initial links. In this chapter we're going to look at maintaining and developing fellowship.

Reflect

How much of a 'buzz' is there in my group? How much is there in my life?

Sharing an interest In his book *The Four Loves,* C S Lewis speaks of friendship as two people (or more) sharing together an interest that others do not share. Fellowship is just Christian jargon for friendship. And trying to 'have fellowship' as an end in itself is almost certainly doomed to failure. Fellowship comes when a group of people share a common interest or activity. That's not to say it comes automatically. Within any common interest group – the local drama society, for example – there will be people who don't get on with one another. It has to be worked at, but without the common interest there is nothing to work at.

The negative side of this is that, in general, the more we concentrate on 'having fellowship' the less fellowship we have! Focus too much on the quality of our relationships and those relationships will start to suffer. Concentrate on studying, working and playing together and those relationships will improve.

What are the common interests that might create fellowship within a small group in the church? There are, of course, some common to the whole church: belief in God, faith in the Lord Jesus Christ, a desire to share the good news with others, the attempt to live a holy, obedient life. Then there are the activities central to the group's existence: prayer and Bible study for a home group, practising and leading worship for a music group, and so on.

Eat, drink and. . . The most basic and popular activity we have in common is eating and drinking. In some groups there's more discussion during the coffee break than in the whole of the rest of the meeting. Balancing a mug of coffee and wondering where to put the biscuit since there's no saucer frees the mind from all those fears which keep us silent when the leader asks, 'Does anyone have anything to say?' and allows us to talk. So, on the subject of refreshments:

- Keep arrangements simple. Don't put too much responsibility onto your host.
- As a leader, circulate to make sure no one is left out and sitting by themselves.
- Don't always stop for coffee at the same point. Look at the programme for the group. Where would an informal break best fit in? With a new group it often helps to start with coffee, so people are relaxed before the group starts.
- If you think discussion on a particular topic is likely to be difficult, bring round the coffee and talk while you're drinking.
- Remember coffee time is not something you do *after* the group is finished; it's a vital part of the group programme.
- By the way, doughnuts with coffee create a better atmosphere than biscuits . . . I don't know why, but try it and see!
- And don't forget to cater for all the different needs in the group. This could mean caffeinated and decaffeinated coffee (should it be 'fair trade'?); tea, fruit tea, squash, cola (can I get away with supermarket brand or does it have to be the real thing?), water (bottled or tap?) and of course at least three kinds of milk – skimmed, semi skimmed and full cream! Is it worth the effort? Yes, it is!

Reflect

How can I use the informality of coffee time to build fellowship within the group?

More eating When we move from coffee and biscuits to eating a meal together then life gets more complicated. The easiest way, if the group can afford it, is to eat out, (or eat in but dial a pizza.) Whether you visit McDonalds, the local pub or a really nice restaurant makes no difference. The important thing is to find a place where people are relaxed and at home . . . even though they're not – if you follow me!

Agapé A common Christian practice for eating together is the Agapé or Lord's Supper. John Mallinson in ***The Small Group Leader*** (see Resources page 6) gives details for holding a full-scale Agape meal. But a very simple celebration of communion can be just as effective. Practical points to consider are:

- **Your church's policy** Who can lead and who can take part? Do you need to invite a minister to lead the communion or can you use a lay person?

The elements   A home-baked loaf or a small bread roll are appropriate. Use the same type of wine as you use in your church communion service, or a red wine or red grape juice.

You can create your own form of service using Scripture passages like 1 Corinthians 11:17–34 or the gospel accounts of the Last Supper; or you can use a service book. This is helpful if you are sharing communion for the first time in a small group and are nervous about 'getting it right'. Take the opportunity of incorporating time to pray for one another during the communion.

It is also possible to re-create a Jewish Passover meal in the group. See **Resources** below for details.

Storytelling   Another common feature useful in building fellowship is the fact that each one of us has a story to tell. The **Ideas** section below gives some suggestions for ways of sharing these stories. You'll find others in a number of the **GROUP FOCUS** sections throughout the book.

Ideas

Play Twenty Questions   A group member thinks of a personal secret. Not a deep, dark secret! But something interesting or amusing about themselves that others are unlikely to know. (A secret I've used is that I was once rescued by a lifeboat.) The rest of the group can ask twenty questions to try and guess the secret, which may only be answered by 'yes' or 'no'.

Show 'n' tell   Each member of the group shows something from their pocket, wallet or handbag and explains how it says something about them.

School memories   With the popularity of the *Friends Reunited* website, talk about school days. What was your best subject? And worst? This works really well when you have a wide age range in the group because schools have changed so much over the years.

'Desert Island Discs'   You don't actually have to play all the music, but each person chooses their eight favourite pieces of music plus a book and a luxury item. Or speed it up by just choosing one piece of music.

Shapes   Give each member of the group a piece of plasticine or modelling clay and ask them to create a shape which says something about them. Talk about the shapes. You can repeat this with shapes which say something about the group or about the church.

Celebrations   Celebrate birthdays, anniversaries, engagements and other significant events in the lives of group members. Whether you have cards, cream cakes or curry(!) don't let these dates pass by unnoticed.

Project   Take on a group project or responsibility. Sponsor a child through a mission agency. Adopt a missionary. Offer to dig a garden or decorate a room or do some other practical task.

Reading/watching together   Agree on a book that all the group will read (or a video or TV programme that all the group will watch at home); then discuss it together. Who enjoyed it? Who hated it? Why? What was moving/striking/disturbing about it?

Practical skill sharing   Read through Exodus 35:25 – 36:1 noting the way people used their skills to build the tabernacle. Think of a project in which the group could use their skills together:

- tapestry, sewing or similar craft
- DIY, carpentry, building or decorating
- gardening, flower arranging
- drama, music, dance or writing

Trips out   A day out, a weekend away or even a week's holiday together will do wonders in building fellowship. But don't try it with a struggling group – it will only exacerbate problems. If you need to keep costs down then the early May Bank Holiday weekend offers (usually) reasonable weather, an extra day away, but pre-season lower prices at hotels, caravan sites, conference centres etc.

See also **Ideas** in chapter 2.

GROUP FOCUS

In pairs, discuss together the person who has made the most impression on you during your life. List the characteristics of this person. How has she/he affected your life? Share some of the discussions with the whole group.

Read   Philippians 2:1–18. Brainstorm: Why has the person of Jesus made such an impact on so many people during the past 2000 years? Why is it that even those who do not become Christians generally speak and think well of him? Pray together. Thank God for Jesus.

If *our attitude should be the same as that of Christ Jesus* (verse 5) what kind of lifestyle should we be striving towards?

Have the following words written on separate cards and share them out among the group:

selfish ambition	vain conceit	humility
putting others first	complaining	arguing
without fault	blameless	pure
shining like stars		

Each person should find where their word appears in the passage to see whether it is something to do or not to do. Then make notes on the cards:

- What is the easiest thing about achieving this?
- What is the most difficult thing about achieving this?
- Where can I get help?

Go round the group sharing answers. What could this group do to help each person try to live like this?

Read 1 Corinthians 13:4–7. Look at the qualities of Christian love mentioned here. Create an imaginary housegroup and some problems and solutions which illustrate these qualities. For example, someone who is always flippant without realising how hurt others are by it. (Love is not rude). Take a few moments to be honest with one another. Which quality do I most need? Pray for one another.

Review

The session had a very practical focus – was this helpful? Were group members able to be honest about the difficulties of reaching the standards set in the Philippians passage?

To think about . . .

The difference between a friend and a fiend is just a letter.

Resources

The Four Loves C S Lewis. Fount. Classic look at affection, friendship, eros (sexual love) and charity.

Finding a Spiritual Friend Timothy Jones. Scripture Union. Designed to help ordinary Christians discover the value of spiritual friendship.

Church: Why Bother? Philip Yancey. Zondervan; **Soul Survivor** Philip Yancey. Hodder and Stoughton. Two books by a best selling author exploring his own journey through life in the church; the harm the church can cause and the way things can be changed so that church becomes life-enhancing.

Church's Ministry Among Jewish People can offer advice in setting up a Passover meal. CMJ, 30c Clarence Road, St Albans, AL1 4JJ. Website:www.cmj.org.uk

Reflect

What have I learned about my relationship with others in the group? About how I can model the life of Jesus as an encouragement to others?

Takeaway

What insights have I gained to help improve the fellowship life of my small group? What ideas do I want to try out? Which ones are not suitable? How appropriate would it be to celebrate communion?

Diary

Week 1 – Raining today so put newspaper down on carpet by door. Made everyone take off shoes and leave them in the hall. Ran round frantically at coffee time so that everyone had little mats (present from Brighton) so their coffee mugs didn't leave rings on the furniture. Bit of a stiff atmosphere.

Week 2 – Got home late from work so didn't have much time to prepare. Kevin and Julie arrived early and helped me set up. They didn't do all the things I do to prevent people messing up the flat. But at the end of the evening there wasn't as much mess as I'd expected. Had really good chat with Don and Maggie who helped with washing up.

Week 3 – Several people came straight from work without eating and at end of study someone suggested we got fish and chips in from the shop round the corner. Before I could mention the problem of cleaning up grease spots it was agreed. While Ross and I were out buying the chips, the others pushed all the furniture back against the wall. We all sat on the floor to eat our chips – out of paper! Although I offered plates. I've never eaten like that before in my life. Conversation was hilarious.

8 Caring in Small Groups

Helping in the ups and downs of life

- 'I was ill, things were going wrong and no one from the church visited me.'
- 'Well, who did you tell that you needed a visit?'
- 'I didn't tell anybody, but someone should have realised.'

Ever had that sort of conversation? Here's another one you might have experienced:

- 'I shared it with the housegroup and the next thing I knew the minister came to visit. I didn't realise that everything I said would be *reported* back.'

Reflect

How well do I balance confidentiality and caring? Do I have a tendency to gossip about members of my group? Alternatively, do I forget all about my group between one meeting and the next?

When it comes to pastoral care it often seems as if you can't win. Which is why it's vital that any small group whose members want to show practical care and concern for one another need to be clear on the ground rules. These may vary from group to group but you'll find it helpful to consider these two:

- Never make a promise of *absolute* confidentiality. In general everyone should agree not to talk about other members outside the group (this includes matters shared for prayer which shouldn't be passed on to others without permission). But, as leader, make it clear that there may occasionally be issues raised which you will need to discuss with the church leadership.
- It is not the place of group members to judge one another. The aim should always be to put yourself in the other person's shoes – to try and understand how they feel and why they are dealing with an issue the way they are.

Here's an example: Julie shares with the group that her son and his girlfriend are coming to stay. They want to share a room while they are visiting. The group could:

- tell Julie that it's sinful to sleep together when you're not married and that she must under no circumstances allow it.
- help Julie to talk, think and pray through the issues involved which might include her feelings about compromising her own Christian moral standards; her worry about alienating her son and breaking her relationship with him; plus a whole package of issues which all Christian parents face about their children growing up and not becoming Christians, not adopting the values of their parents.

Reflect

How quick am I to judge? How ready am I to try and put myself into someone else's shoes?

The group and the church   It is essential to be clear about how pastoral care in the small group relates to the overall pastoral care of the church. If someone is ill, members of the small group might well visit. But will the vicar, minister or elder be told and be expected to visit? Church leaders are not psychic, they need to be told when people are ill. Who will follow up major problems or matters which affect other parts of the life of the church?

It may be helpful if the pastoral responsibility for the small group is given to someone other than the person who leads the session. This will help avoid putting too much work on individuals. It's also true that the gifts necessary to lead a small group study are not necessarily those needed to offer pastoral care and vice versa.

It is vital that groups do not attempt to take responsibility for areas of pastoral care which need professional help. Most groups would not attempt to treat medical illnesses or perform an operation on a member. Neither should they try to deal with:

- long term depression
- mental illness
- drug addiction
- abuse and violence

Prayerful and practical assistance can be offered, but never suggest that these things can simply be kept within the group. Those involved should be encouraged to seek professional help and given support through that process. It may in some cases be helpful for the leader to discuss with a professional counsellor the kind of help that is most appropriate for the group to offer.

Look after yourself   However 'temptation proof' you think you are, when counselling or caring for group members, don't put yourself into a situation where you are alone with someone of the opposite sex; or get yourself into any situation which could easily be misunderstood.

Those who offer pastoral care to others should always have opportunity to meet with a church leader (or other appropriate person) for a regular debriefing session. This can be used to talk through issues that have arisen, to pray together and for the church leader to ensure that group leaders are not taking too much of the pastoral care problems on themselves personally.

When problems go on and on The most difficult issues to deal with pastorally are the long term ones. It's easy to be really enthusiastic about praying for someone and offering practical help through a short illness or other problem. But what happens when the sick person doesn't get better? What happens when the person who has lost a job just doesn't seem able to find another?

Some ways forward:

- Remind the group that prayer is not magic nor is it a demand that God must fulfil. The fact that healing doesn't come or a problem isn't solved does not necessarily mean that there is something wrong with our prayers. Explore the place of fasting alongside prayer but remember that fasting doesn't guarantee 'results' either. Long term suffering is a real test of our understanding of the sovereignty of God.
- Remember that one of the fruits of the Spirit (Galatians 5:22) is patience (literally longsuffering). The test of our love is that we go on caring.
- Revise the ways in which you pray and offer help. It's not usually possible to sustain short term levels of prayer and support over a long period, but you do need to show the person in need that you haven't given up or forgotten them.

Ideas

There are many organisations, Christian and otherwise, offering training in counselling and pastoral care at various levels. Encourage those who are gifted in these areas to pursue as much training as they can.

If there is opportunity to run a 'listening' course, this will be of value to all group members.

Are there any in the group who have expertise relating to pastoral care? People who work in medicine, counselling, etc? Get them to share their experiences with the group. Similarly, if any have experience such as caring for an elderly parent or working as foster parents or have experienced bereavement or life threatening illness, then create opportunities for them to share their experiences with the group. Caution: only ask people to share personal experiences which are some way in the past. Give people time to come to terms with their experience before asking them to talk about it.

GROUP FOCUS

In this study we're going to look at four scenarios which represent some of the pastoral needs which might be experienced by members of a small group. In all four cases there are no absolute right answers. Passages of Scripture which relate to the need are suggested but these need to be applied in the light of individual circumstances.

Before getting into these scenarios, spend a few minutes in pairs sharing the best advice and the worst advice you've ever been given. The best of these can be shared with the whole group.

1 Betty is 77 years old. She has lived alone since her husband died and is fiercely independent. She is not always easy to get on with. In recent months her eyesight has been failing and she has become less mobile. It's getting harder for her to do her own shopping, cooking and cleaning. She comes regularly to the housegroup but seldom shares much about her own needs. What can the group do to show they care? Starting points: Acts 6:1–7; 1 Timothy 5:1–10; James 1:27. What other passages are helpful?

2 Franklin is very unhappy at work. One or two people there, who know he is a Christian, make his life a misery by name-calling, leaving pornographic magazines on his desk and generally trying to get him to lose his temper. When he responds they tell him that Christians are supposed to forgive people. Franklin has had interviews for jobs elsewhere but not been able to obtain another position. What can the group do to show that they care? Starting points: Psalm 10; Matthew 5:43–48; Ephesians 6:10–20. What other passages are helpful?

3 Mark and Claire have two teenage sons. Paul, the older, is studying for his A levels and seems to be working hard and getting good results. There are stories in the church that he has been seen out clubbing some weekends, sometimes quite drunk, but his parents seem to know nothing about this, believing him to be spending the weekend with a friend from church. Stephen, the younger, wants to drop out of school as soon as he is 16, move out from home and get a flat with some friends. His parents are very worried about what he'll get up to, although so far he has not shown any inclination to get into trouble. What can the group do to show that they care? Starting points: Ephesians 6:1–4; Luke 15:11–32; 1 Corinthians 13:4–7. What other passages are helpful?

4 Zara wants to go to Bible College. She is convinced that God is calling her to some sort of ministry. One of the reasons she is so convinced is that she has had six jobs in the past five years and hasn't been able to stick with any of them. This, she believes, is God closing doors and calling her out into ministry. She has no savings to help cover the cost of college. She does have some gifts in working with children and young people, in speaking, and in getting alongside the older people in the church. She is 24 years old and single. What can the group do to show they care? Starting points: Isaiah 6:1–13; Acts 13:1–3; 1 Timothy 3. What other passages are helpful?

Review

How well did the group relate to the four scenarios? Did it help to have some Scripture verses given as starting points? Were the group able to find other relevant verses? How easy was it to relate the Bible verses to contemporary situations?

To think about . . .

'Nurture means growth not only in knowing the Lord and in doing his will, but in *being like him*.' **The Church** E P Clowney. IVP.

Resources

Mentoring   John Mallinson. Scripture Union. Practical guide to mentoring as a part of Christian discipleship.

In the Palm of God's Hand   Wendy Bray. Bible Reading Fellowship. The diary of a mother of two children who is undergoing treatment for cancer. Very helpful in seeing how she perceives the care (and lack of care) offered by her church.

Anchored in the Storm   Irene Howat. Christian Focus. Twelve true stories of Christians who have experienced great trials and found comfort in God.

Where is God When It Hurts?   Philip Yancey. Marshall Pickering. Yancey explores the reality of pain; how it works and why God tolerates it. A useful book for leaders but also one which could helpfully be given to people going through difficult times.

The Problem of Pain   C S Lewis. Fount; ***A Grief Observed*** C S Lewis. Faber. Two older books; the first Lewis's classic apologetic and the second a personal account of his own bereavement.

Skilful Shepherds   Derek Tidball. IVP. For leaders who want to go deeper. Explores pastoral theology; the need for those who pastor to have a good grasp of Christian doctrine and a wide range of skills.

The Sacred Diary of Adrian Plass   Adrian Plass. Marshall Pickering. I've mentioned this book before but in this context read the entries from April 24th when Adrian decides to put himself 'entirely at the disposal of the members of [his] study group' to May 16th when he meets an abandoned family at Humph's café. Better than a text-book.

The Road through the Desert   Alison Jacobs. Bible Reading Fellowship. A series of personal Bible readings following Moses through the desert, which could helpfully be given to group members going through their own wilderness experiences.

SPCK in their ***Sheldon Press*** list have a large range of books dealing with specific medical, psychological and pastoral problems. Send for a catalogue to SPCK, Holy Trinity Church, Marylebone Road, London, NW1 4DU. These titles may be helpful in giving information about specific subjects, but beware of the danger of thinking you are an expert because you've read a book!

Reflect

What areas in my own life make me vulnerable in helping others? What areas in my own life give me insight into other people's needs?

Takeaway

How would the scenarios approach work with my small group? What have I learned that will help me improve pastoral care for my group?

Diary

Phil – starts new job, Monday.

Amber – exams this week.

Stacie – mum's not well. Away next week?

Talk to Nilay about Peter.

Nasreen's kids – promised to pray.

Neil – help move in furniture/redecorating.

Glad I'm not a pastor or counsellor. It's hard enough just praying for people and giving them a helping hand!

9 Growing the Group

Developing the empty chair mentality

One of the strengths of the small group system is that it allows the formation of a close, intimate group where every member can feel at home. One of the weaknesses of the small group system is that it allows the formation of a close, intimate group where every member can feel at home. It's so easy to move from being at home with one another to being shut away from the rest of the world. 'This is our group. We don't want any outsiders!' If a small group is to remain healthy it needs to be open to new people joining, and it needs to be aware of, and have a concern for, the community. In this chapter we'll look at ways the group can be always ready to welcome newcomers. In the next we'll consider ways it can actively reach into the community.

A good basic principle for a small group of the fellowship/ prayer/study type is that there should always be an empty chair. You could do this literally as a powerful reminder every time you meet, or just keep it as a symbol in your minds. An empty chair means the group is always ready to welcome an extra member. (For what to do when the group gets too big see chapter 14).

How can you grow your small group? The simple answer is by inviting other people along. Obvious 'targets' are:

- other church 'regulars' who don't attend small groups
- people on the fringe of the church
- family, friends and neighbours who don't come to church at all

'But, hang on, in our small group we pray and study the Bible. It wouldn't be suitable for people who aren't already Christians.' Don't be so sure! Non-Christians are not stupid. Like all of us they learn to adapt to new situations. They get to know how a group works if:

- they are made welcome
- the group makes an effort to make them feel at home
- the group explains the way things are done
- the group doesn't pressure them to believe but lets them move at their own pace

There are many people in our churches whose journey to faith has been through belonging to a small group.

If being open to others is going to be part of the culture and ethos of your group then:

- encourage group members to think about people they could invite
- pray for those people who are inviting and being invited
- don't all bring someone new along at once; try to introduce new people into the group one at a time, but keep the empty chair mentality

Reflect

Do I feel so at home with my group that I don't want others to come and spoil it?

New people – new ideas New people often bring new ideas to the group. Some will be welcomed, some will not.

One of the easiest ways to make a new person feel really unwelcome is to constantly reject their ideas and suggestions.

- Try to create the kind of atmosphere in the group where new ideas are always listened to; nothing should be rejected out of hand.
- Be grateful and positive towards people who come up with new ideas.
- If an idea can't be introduced completely, consider ways in which it can be partly introduced or adapted.
- Don't be afraid to experiment; if someone suggests a new way of doing things that the group is not sure about, try it out and evaluate how things went.

Ideas

Get the group to brainstorm all the different people they meet in a typical week. In pairs each person can work through the list and try and identify someone they think might be interested in coming along. Each pair agrees to pray for the people they have identified until a suitable opportunity arises to invite them to the group.

If newcomers to the group are not familiar with handling the Bible, make sure you use page numbers as well as Bible references. Unfortunately this won't work if everyone has a different edition of the Bible! In this case give some clues 'Psalms – almost exactly in the middle', 'Revelation – last book in the Bible' etc. From time to time point out the contents page – it's surprising how many of us don't think about it even when we're totally lost looking for a minor prophet or wondering if Ecclesiastes is one of Paul's letters.

If you're studying one of the gospels why not get a copy of the gospel for each member of the group to make it easier to follow?

Listen to what newcomers have to say. Don't be too quick to give them the approved Christian answer to their questions. Try to see things through their eyes.

When someone is there for the first time, explain what prayer is and how you pray. Make it clear that it's not compulsory for everyone to join in – or to 'put their hands together and close their eyes', but it's OK just to sit and listen.

Make a list of things you say without explanation because you assume everyone in the group understands them. Some examples: 'Let's have a time of worship'; 'We'll have a prayer time now'; 'We'll read round the passage.' How many need explanation to a newcomer?

Imagine you are completely new to a small group. What are the questions you might ask?

Don't assume that non-Christians don't have valid things to say about the Bible. This is wrong theologically – if God can speak through a donkey or use a pagan king he can certainly speak through your next door neighbour. It's also helpful to hear how someone who hasn't been brought up in our own tradition sees things. It challenges and sharpens our own thinking and sometimes exposes the fact that we haven't really thought about some issues at all.

Do icebreakers break the ice? Icebreakers are those games which people use to start a group and which range from silly to incredibly embarrassing. If you decide to use icebreakers, think carefully about your group. Watch how they respond. Adapt the type of icebreakers you use accordingly.

GROUP FOCUS

Read John 1:35–51. In pairs discuss: If you had been Andrew or Philip and had met with Jesus, who, from among people you know today, would you have brought to meet Jesus?

As a whole group list the reasons why it is difficult to invite family, friends, colleagues, neighbours to church activities. What in general could be done to make it easier? What specifically could the small group do to make it easier for members to bring others along?

Design a simple card which explains what the group is, where it meets and what it does, which could be given as an invitation.

In pairs, share situations where you have been a newcomer to a group (it need not be a church group). Were you made to feel at home? What things did you find difficult? What things were helpful? Together draw up a list of characteristics of a welcoming group. How well do your groups match up to these characteristics?

Read Hebrews 13:2. What are the benefits of welcoming strangers? Share the following passages out:

Genesis 18
Genesis 19:1–29
Genesis 32:22–32
Joshua 5:13 – 6:5
Judges 6:1–24

Judges 13:2–25
Matthew 25:35.

Ask people in twos or threes to read the story and then:

- briefly retell the story to the rest of the group
- explain the effects of entertaining an 'angel unawares'
- pick out any parallels with welcoming strangers into a small group

Using a concordance, check out what the Bible has to say about strangers. How many times are strangers mentioned? What reasons are given for being hospitable to strangers?

Design (it doesn't matter if you're not artistic) a series of posters which could be used to promote the biblical ideas you've uncovered. Since 'strangers' has a negative connotation – as in 'children shouldn't go with strangers' – what better word could you use?

Spread out the posters (even if they're only roughly drawn) and use them as a focus for prayer.

To think about . . .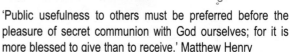

'Public usefulness to others must be preferred before the pleasure of secret communion with God ourselves; for it is more blessed to give than to receive.' Matthew Henry

Resources

Lost for Words James Lawrence. Bible Reading Fellowship. Looks at the ways we can share our faith naturally with friends, colleagues and family.

Reflect

How comfortable am I about new people coming into the group? Do I worry that they may upset the group? Challenge my authority? Know more than I do?

Takeaway

How do we encourage people to think about inviting others to the group? How do we make the group ready to receive others and welcome them?

Diary

Week 1 – Made sure there was one more chair than we needed (just as we'd been told to do) but Jez brought along a friend I hadn't expected, so we didn't have an empty chair after all.

Week 2 – Put out two extra chairs but Jez's friend came again and Rachel brought someone too. How am I going to get this empty chair thing right if they keep bringing new people?

Week 3 – Put out six empty chairs. Three of them were filled and three were empty. Does that make up for two weeks when I didn't have any? And now I've got empty chairs, what do I do with them? I think I'm going to have to have this whole idea explained to me again.

10 Outreach from Groups

Building links into the community

There are many different ways of setting up a small groups network within a church. Groups can be based on age, gender, interest or location. Where they are based on location then there are opportunities to reach out into the community. (This may also be possible where there is another basis for the group structure, but it is not so obvious.) The theory is that each small group is made up of people who live in a certain area and the group meets in a home in that area and therefore has an interest in and responsibility for that area. In practice, this doesn't always work out. The mix of members in some groups will not always be viable; some people, for whatever reason, will want to meet with a group which isn't their area or community group. But whatever the flaws, basing small groups geographically does offer opportunity for outreach.

Where groups are not organised according to where people live it may still be possible for groups to 'adopt' the community where they meet or to look at outreach in terms of reaching non-church family and work colleagues.

In the previous chapter we looked at the very simple approach of inviting individuals into the small group. In this chapter we'll look at special events and activities with an evangelistic edge.

Reflect

How much hunger does my group have to see non-Christians come to faith? Would we prefer the group to stay comfortable, meeting our needs and not worrying about others?

> A small group of people from
> ABC Church meet in this area
> to pray and study the Bible.
> We'd like to pray for you.
> If you have a specific need which
> you'd like us to pray about
> jot down the details
> in complete confidence
> and return this card to:
>
> _____
> _____
> _____
> _____

Plan and pray Start your plans for outreach to the local community by praying for that community. Put a map in the centre of the group. Mark out the area you consider 'yours' and brainstorm what you know about it before praying for it. Then arrange to go out and prayer walk the area. At its simplest level, prayer walking is simply a way of seeing the needs of an area and being prompted (by your own observation and

by the Holy Spirit) to pray about things you'd never think about while sitting indoors. Go out in twos or threes. Walk along the streets. As you see things which prompt you to pray then pray aloud; talk to God exactly as you talk to the people you are walking with. It's not embarrassing (well, not very) and other people you pass have no idea you're praying – they think you're talking to a friend (which of course you are). After the prayer walk share the thoughts and impressions which have come to you.

In all probability most of the people who live in your community have no idea that a small group from the church meets here. Why should they? So you need to create some awareness. Your next step could be to print a simple card similar to the one shown in the column opposite. You're unlikely to receive a huge response but you will have introduced yourself to the area and, in general, people in the community will appreciate your offer to pray. You can repeat this once or twice a year.

What sort of events? Think very carefully about the area you live in and about your own small group before planning outreach. You may find it helpful to look at statistics held by your local council or local library about the make-up of the area; talk to your local councillor about current issues; or even undertake your own survey. You want to make sure:

- the group is able to think through practical ways of being salt and light in the community
- any event fits the community you're in – do people in your area have cocktail parties or barbecues or take away pizzas?
- any event is within the capability of the group; don't take on events that are too ambitious or demanding

Ideas

 Get involved in local events (street parties, carnival, protest over planning issues etc) before inviting people to join your group.

Run a simple fund-raising event for a local charity as a way of building bridges into the community.

If you are running any event at which there will be Christian input (speaker, testimony, video etc) then make sure this is clear in your invitation. People object strongly to being 'conned' or 'having religion forced on them'.

Food-related activities are always popular and there's plenty of choice: coffee morning, barbecue, formal meal, supper, breakfast. Use a home or a local café.

Make links with your local school. Can members of the group help on the PTA, serve as governors or become parent helpers? There may be opportunities to speak in a lesson or take an assembly (but take advice and training from someone who already visits schools first.) Make the school, its staff and pupils and all its needs part of the prayer life of the group.

GROUP FOCUS

Go round the group and briefly share the ways in which each person came to faith. What common factors are there in the different accounts?

Have a selection of popular magazines and newspapers available and use them to build up a picture of what the typical non-Christian believes and holds dear. Try and create a non-Christian creed which you think would be widely acceptable. If you want to follow this up afterwards, turn the creed into a questionnaire and use it to find out what friends, colleagues etc really believe.

Be silent for a minute or two and reflect on contemporary society. Ask yourself how you feel about it. Share answers within the group.

Read Acts 17:16–34. Talk your way through the passage:

- verse 16 – How 'distressed' am I about the culture around me? How big a part does that culture play in my life?
- verse 18 – Do people want to debate with us? How do people misunderstand the message we try to share?
- verses 22,23 – What are the contemporary starting points for communicating with our society?
- verses 24–28 – What arguments are most effective in communicating the gospel?
- verse 28 – What helpful cultural references and illustrations can we use?
- verse 32 – What do non-Christians find the biggest stumbling blocks? How can we overcome them?
- verse 34 – What measure of 'success' should we expect in our outreach?

Put together the group members' stories of coming to faith and the discussion on Acts 17 and try to develop a list of practical ways in which small groups in the church can engage in effective outreach. Who would they try to reach? What methods would they use? What resources would they need? Pray for people in the communities where your small groups meet.

Review

How effective was the exercise in drawing up a non-Christian creed in helping the group enter into contemporary culture? Did the group find it easy to relate the situation in Athens 2000 years ago to society today?

To think about . . .

'"If religion is the opium of the people, Christianity is the paracetemol!" claimed a critic of the church recently. One of the biggest mistakes the church has made is to create and then consistently to reinforce the popular idea that Christianity is boring.' Steve Chalke in the foreword to *Evangelism Made Slightly Less Difficult*   Nick Pollard, IVP.

Resources

50 Easy Outreach Ideas   Paul Mogford. Kingsway. Events which can be easily organised and maximise opportunities to build friendships.

100 Instant Faith Sharing Talks   Ian Knox. Kingsway. Outline talks for every sort of evangelistic occasion.

Thank God It's Monday   Mark Greene. Scripture Union. Making the most of the time we spend at work.

Friendship Matters   David Spriggs and Darrell Jackson. Scripture Union. The vital role of friendship in evangelism.

Sharing the Salt   Ida Glaser & Shaylesh Raja. Scripture Union. Building positive relationships with people of other faiths.

Man to Man   Stephen Croft. Scripture Union. Sharing faith with men through friendship, in church and society.

Wake Up to Work   Geoff Shattock. Scripture Union. Developing relationships in the workplace.

Using the Bible in Evangelism   Derek Tidball. Bible Society. Out of print but worth looking for. Does exactly what the title says.

Finding Faith Today   John Finney. Bible Society. Fascinating research (1992) on how adults come to faith.

Reflect

What do we need to learn in order to be salt and light in the community? Are we part of the local community or just a group which happens to meet there? How can we become more a part of that community?

Takeaway

Do I have the gifts and skills to lead the group in evangelism or should I be identifying someone else in the group to take a lead? What is the next stage for my group in reaching out into the community?

Diary

Leave note for milkman

Book hairdressing appointment

Water plants for Jane while away

Take novel to work to lend Farid

Book baby sitter

Ring for pizza delivery

Ask woman across road to feed cat next weekend

Have to make a list for housegroup of non-Christians I'm in contact with. But I just don't know any!

11 All-Age Groups

When crossing the barriers is worthwhile

'Why on earth would we want an all-age group? Our small group meets in the evenings – when the children are in bed – and it's for serious prayer and Bible study. Kids would ruin it!'

I'm not suggesting that *all* small groups in the church should be all-age groups. But there are times when all-age groups can offer exciting new insights to young and old.

For example, you can use all-age small groups:

- as part of a family service
- on conferences and house parties alongside the times when children and young people go into age-specific groups
- as part of special events specifically designed to bring the whole church family together

Why would you want to have all-age groups? Some of the biblical reasons you'll find below in the **GROUP FOCUS** material. And here are some others:

- **The young valued** It makes children and young people feel valued and part of the church. Why do young people so frequently drift away from the church? Often because they were never made to feel part of it in the first place.
- **Older people gain** Older people can learn, even from young children, and benefit from exploring again the simplicity of faith.
- **Everyone challenged** A mix of ages and experience in a small group challenges what we think we understand. Both those older and those younger than us will see things in a different way.
- **It's fun!** Having children and young people in a small group liberates us to try some activities we've always fancied but been too embarrassed to suggest in a group of 'grown ups'.

Important All-age activities are *not* children's activities with adults joining in with embarrassment! The aim is always to have content which is significant and relevant to all ages in a format in which all ages can take part.

In particular don't underestimate children. With help and appropriate methods they are well able to grasp (at their own level) theological concepts like sin, redemption, salvation, holiness etc. They can worship 'in Spirit and in truth'. They can pray – and their faith in prayer will sometimes shame our adult 'safety first' mentality.

A small boy was heard praying over a packet of breakfast cereal. His mother asked what he was doing. 'I'm praying that there will be a Jimmy Neutron figure in the packet.' His mother started to explain that this is not the sort of thing to pray about but he interrupted her by saying, 'We were told in church that if you really want something, you should ask God for it.' There are two approaches to this sort of childhood naivety. One is to

tell kids that there are things we pray about and things we don't. That approach, I suggest, is unhelpful and unbiblical. The better approach is to encourage all genuine examples of faith and prayer and then to help children work through the issue if the prayer is not answered, or not answered in the way they expect. (There was no Jimmy Neutron figure in the box!)

All-age activities should aim to stretch children and help adults become child-like – not childish. See Matthew 18:3.

Finally Keep it short. Don't let any individual activity run on for too long. Don't have too long between drink and toilet breaks. But don't make breaks too long either. Keep the programme moving – all ages will appreciate that.

Reflect

Do I believe that God can speak through a child? Do I believe that as the family of God we can all relate together across age barriers?

Ideas

Here's an outline for an all-age programme. The individual parts of the programme can, of course, be used in other settings and the techniques can be applied to other Bible passages and themes.

Start by giving each person a People Bingo card in the style of the one below. Adjust the contents to suit the group you have. The idea is to move around the room finding people who fit each category and getting them to sign the box. No signatures should be repeated.

Had cornflakes for breakfast	Owns a rabbit	Rides a bike
Owns a PlayStation	Uses nail varnish	Was alive during the Second World War
Has grandparents who are alive	Has grandchildren	Doesn't like chocolate
Listens to Radio 4	Knows what is currently number one in the charts	Goes to school

Ask people to arrange themselves in groups of eight in which there is at least an eight year age gap between each member of the group and no two members of the group come from the same family. You may need to be flexible about both requirements according to the make-up of your group and depending on whether young children can or should be in a group without their parents.

Talk together in each group about what Christians believe. Allow the youngest to go first. Write each suggestion on a separate piece of paper. When you have a comprehensive range of beliefs spread them out on the floor or a large table. Together try and sort them out. Which are the really important ones – the ones of which you could say: 'You can't really be a Christian without believing this.'? Having picked these out, arrange them in some sort of logical order. Appoint a scribe with a flip chart headed 'We believe . . .' to list these key beliefs.

Using as wide a range of art and craft materials as you can muster, working in pairs, create a visual representation of each of the beliefs. The end of this activity would be a good time to break for cola and chocolate. (For an all-age activity this beats tea and biscuits hands down!)

During the break, everyone should take time to look at the displays produced.

After the break, each group should be given a simple song, rhyme or tune. This could be a children's song or nursery rhyme, a current pop song or a TV theme tune. The task for each group is to turn their creed into a song or poem following the pattern they have been given. It can be as simple or as complex as they wish. For example, based on *Frère Jacques* you might start:

We believe, we believe:
God's our dad, God's our dad.
Jesus is our brother, Jesus is our brother.
Holy Spirit,
Fills our lives.

When all the groups have finished then a small group – of all ages – can prepare an act of worship for everyone together which will use these creations and other elements which have been prepared beforehand. This might be a good time to allow children to play a fairly active game (watched and cheered by the adults) followed by a quiet game, before the final act of worship together.

Review

How would members of the church respond to an all-age programme like this? Which elements of the programme would be most effective? Which elements would be least likely to work?

GROUP FOCUS

Ask group members to imagine that they could stay at one particular age for ever. What age would it be and why?

3	no responsibilities
5	the world's opening up before me
10	so much to discover, so much to do
14	running wild, life is great
18	grown up!
25	the world's my oyster
35	at my peak
40	when life begins
50	wisdom and maturity
65	time to relax
80	glad to be alive

Each person shares with the group one characteristic of their present age which they're really glad about and one they could do without. Use these to pray for one another.

Read Proverbs 17:6. Choose which animal gives the best picture of children in the church.

kittens	playful and active
puppies	eager to please
lion cubs	great potential to grow into
wild horses	difficult to control, but lots to give
chicks	needing a lot of care
ugly ducklings	but swans one day
parrots	never stop talking

How can we build relationships in the church in such a way that older people delight in the young and the young take a pride in the older people? Take time to pray for God to bridge the age gaps in the church.

Read 1 John 2:9–17. John addresses people in different stages of life. List some of the virtues of different ages and some of the dangers.

	virtues	dangers
childhood		
youth		
middle age		
old age		

How do we learn to love and care for people of all ages? Does it always have to be in separate, age-specific groups?

How do we help to protect one another from the pressures of the world?

Pray for individuals of different ages within the church.

John constantly refers to the Christians he is writing to as *children*. Divide the group into pairs or threes. Give each of them one of the five chapters in 1 John and ask them to note all the references to children. Then together answer the questions:

- Whose children are we?
- How are we to behave?
- What do we receive from our Father?
- What dangers face us?
- What are the blessings of being children of God?
- How can we help all ages in the church to enjoy being children of God?

Review

How helpful was it to have sheets of answers to choose from? How well did the discussion and prayer interrelate? Did the prayer sharpen the focus of the discussion? How would adults in the church respond to using all-age small groups in, say, a day conference or weekend event?

Resources

A Church for All Ages   Peter Graystone and Eileen Turner. Scripture Union. An excellent book which I use regularly. The first half gives helpful guidance and the second a great range of resources for all-age prayer and worship.

All Together Now   Christine Wright. Scripture Union. Photocopiable resources for all-age worship.

100 Instant Ideas for All-Age Worship   Sue Relf. Kingsway. Pick and mix ideas for all-age worship.

Special Event For All the Church Family; All-Age Activities for Learning and Worship   Michael Lush.

Scripture Union. Two books of practical resources. Long out of print but copies still available from Christian Resources Project, 14 Lipson Rd, Plymouth, PL4 8PW.

Count Us In   NCEC. Resources for all-age worship.

Heirs Together   Daphne Kirk. Kevin Mayhew Publishers. An introduction to the principles for establishing inter-generational cell church. Kevin Mayhew publishes a range of inter-generational cell church resources. Catalogue from Kevin Mayhew, Buxhall, Stowmarket, Suffolk, IP14 3BW.

To think about . . .

Preacher Charles Spurgeon tells of 'two little boys who were one day asked if they would like to go to Heaven, and who . . . said that they really should not. When they were asked "Why not?" one of them replied, "I should not like to go to Heaven because grandpa would be there, and he would be sure to say, "Get along, boys; be off with you!"'

Reflect

What have I learned about what I can give as part of God's family? What I can receive from others in God's family?

Takeaway

What practical and organisational problems are there in running an all-age programme in my church? What issues need to addressed concerning people's perception of all-age activities?

My diary – Jon aged 8

Went to church even though it was Saturday. Lots of people were there. Had to be in a group with really old people. A lady told me about when she was eight. It was hundreds of years ago and her school was really different from mine. They had to eat cabbage and they got the cane for talking in class!!!! She believed in Jesus when she was eight and said he has looked after her ever since. I want him to look after me.

Diary – Jackie aged 37

Never would have believed it. James and Chloe both had a great time at the family day at church. I was so afraid they'd run riot. But Mrs Green and old Tom Hand were just brilliant with them. Really treated them as if they were normal human beings!

Diary – Vera aged 80

Isn't God good to bring so many young people and families into the church. I nearly cried when little Nasreen talked about praying for her baby brother when he was ill. And those teenagers! Their hair and clothes may be funny but the way they stand up for what they believe among their friends at school! I've put them all on my prayer list.

12 Groups Meeting to do Business

Towards more effective committees

The PCC, diaconate and church committee are all small groups. How can they function more effectively? When we have a business meeting, we usually work according to a certain formula. We call it 'the agenda' and it usually starts with prayer followed by apologies, minutes, matters arising and then the various items of business. It can be a helpful and efficient way of dealing with business items in a methodical way. Or it can be a straightjacket which hinders people saying what they really feel, and prevents the whole group hearing what God has to say. How can we make our business meetings more responsive to God, more user-friendly to committee members, and more effective in achieving their purposes?

Make prayer and worship real Many meetings in a Christian setting start with a word of Scripture, a 'blessed thought' and a prayer. While meant sincerely, this often becomes little more than a formality. Here are some different approaches to think about:

- Allow sufficient time for prayer and worship. I'm not suggesting that every business meeting becomes a Bible study group, but instead of two to three minutes allow ten to fifteen minutes.
- Choose Scripture to read which is relevant to the business agenda. If you're about to tackle the church budget then look at some of the Bible's teaching on money. Think and pray about the theological issues before you attempt to deal with practical issues.
- Involve the whole group in prayer if possible. Don't make it simply another job the chairman always does.
- Listen for what God has to say!
- It may be better in some cases not to spend time at the start of the meeting but to link prayer and Scripture to a specific item on the agenda. For example, if you're moving from a detailed account of the problems with the drains to considering someone who feels a call to serve with a mission organisation, it will help to take time between the two items to pray and read together. (If the drains are always on the agenda it might be helpful to make them a focus for prayer too!)

Plan the priorities It probably does make sense to start with apologies, minutes and matters arising but the next item of business should be the most important. When you put routine business near the top of an agenda, people will speak at length on trivial topics. When it's at the end, the desire to go home focuses the mind wonderfully.

Think about techniques The kind of techniques that have been used throughout this book for Bible study can also be effectively used in a business meeting. For example:

- When approaching a new topic, start by brainstorming. Get everyone to call out relevant words without thinking too deeply. Have someone write them all down on a flip chart. When there are a lot of words, look at them together and try to group them. From the groupings, develop topics which need to be considered.
- Instead of sharing ideas verbally, use a large sheet of paper which covers the whole table and have everyone write ideas on it. Then move round the table looking at what's been written. Again group ideas and develop topics for further consideration.
- When lots of information has to be considered, give out written reports well in advance of the meeting. Don't then go through the whole paper at the meeting but ask people to make marks in the margin like this:
  - ? I need more information.
  - * I am not happy with this.
  - ! I don't understand this.

  Discuss these items rather than spending time covering ground which everyone is happy with.
- Discuss some issues in pairs or sub groups who can report back to the whole committee.
- Look back to chapter 3. The technique used in the **GROUP FOCUS** to look at a moral or ethical issue can also be used to explore a practical issue.
- Vary the way you pray in the business meeting. Any of the ideas in chapter 5 could be used.
- Don't forget the coffee. A strategic break for coffee and doughnuts can refresh the brain, ease tensions and give time to reflect.
- Pastoral issues often generate a lot of tension because of the personalities involved. Before discussing the specific case, investigate issues in a neutral way using scenarios as in chapter 8.

Know what you are trying to achieve Here are some reasons for changing the format of business meetings:

- enable group members to have more sense of the presence of God both in the mundane and the significant work of the church
- enable discussion to flow more freely
- help people listen to each other
- facilitate better understanding of the subject under discussion
- prevent unnecessary conflict and tension
- help the group make the best decisions

But remember – 'If it ain't broke – don't fix it!'

GROUP FOCUS

Think of a business meeting which takes place in the church. Together as a group work out a typical agenda.

Read Acts 13:1–3. Was this a business meeting or a prayer meeting? Certainly a very important piece of business was transacted. What place do prayer, Bible study, and fasting have in your business agenda? How can we ensure that Scripture and prayer aren't token gestures or simply the way we always start or close our meetings? How would you answer this: 'If we spend more time in prayer we won't have enough time to deal with the agenda.'?

Read Acts 15:1–35 which is printed at the end of this chapter. Underline different parts of the passage in different colours.

- blue: the issue being addressed
- red: Scripture used in coming to a decision
- yellow: evidence/testimony presented
- black: the role of leaders
- green: the decision reached
- brown: action taken

In the margins around the passage write your own comments about how the meeting was conducted. Here is a meeting which could have split the church in two. What lessons are there for the way in which we handle sensitive issues which have the potential to divide the church? (In the training course each participant has a copy of this book to mark up. When using this technique in other groups you can ask members to mark their own Bibles, photocopy Bible text – perhaps enlarging it – or retype Bible text and copy.)

Imagine you're a first-century Christian. How would you have reacted to this meeting and its decision if you had been:

- a converted Pharisee?
- a converted Gentile?
- someone who hadn't really thought about the issue before?

Choose a potentially divisive issue: use of tongues in worship; women in leadership; children taking communion – whatever is relevant in your situation. Draw up an agenda for a meeting in which the issue could be discussed.

- What role will the church leaders play?
- What Scriptures will be helpful to look at?
- What evidence/testimony would it be helpful to hear?
- How will you come to a decision?
- How will you communicate and implement that decision?
- Will you deal with the issue in one meeting or would it be better to spread it over a series of meetings?

Reflect

When I am in a meeting with a controversial topic, how well do I listen to others – especially those I disagree with? And how well do I listen to God?

Make a short list of some of the appointments which are made in your church – deacon, caretaker, study group leader, flower arranger etc. Against each one list the qualities you look for in the person appointed.

Read Acts 6:1–7. Draw up a brief job description of the work these seven men were to do. Again list the qualities which (if the job were being done today) you would look for. Look at the qualities specified in the passage. Are these included in your list – or in the lists for the other jobs you've considered? Why were they needed for what is basically a pretty ordinary job – 'waiting on tables'?

Review

How well did the underlining with coloured pens focus attention on the procedure followed in the meeting? Did the group find it easy to put themselves into the position of first-century Christians? Did Acts 6 challenge any preconceptions about the qualifications required for different sorts of jobs?

To think about . . .

'Committee: the unwilling picked by the unfit to do the unnecessary for the ungrateful.' (Anon)

Resources

How to Develop the Spirituality of your Church David Spriggs. Administry.

Parkinson's Law C N Parkinson. New edition from Penguin 2002. Readily available in libraries. The perfect not-too-serious read for anyone battling with bureaucracy. Some fascinating insights into how meetings work. Parkinson's most famous law is 'Work expands so as to fill the time available for its completion' but 'The time spent on any item of the agenda will be in inverse proportion to the sum involved' will be a familiar one to most church committee members.

Reflect

Do I go to business meetings ready to listen to other people? Do I go to business meetings expecting to hear God speak? How can I worship and serve God in discussing the mundane everyday life of the church?

Takeaway

What changes might be made to business meetings in my church? What opposition might there be to change? What do we seek to achieve through change?

Diary

Old Jones started the meeting without praying or reading the Bible. Just launched straight into the agenda. Couldn't believe it! But then, he stopped business three times. Once to pray for Jo after we'd appointed her to a new job. Once to pray for the community association who have asked to rent our building and once to pray for wisdom before we discussed the really controversial item on the agenda. Despite this, we managed to finish earlier than usual.

Meeting to do Business – Acts 15:1–35

Some men came down from Judea to Antioch and were teaching the brothers: 'Unless you are circumcised, according to the custom taught by Moses, you cannot be saved.' This brought Paul and Barnabas into sharp dispute and debate with them. So Paul and Barnabas were appointed, along with some other believers, to go up to Jerusalem to see the apostles and elders about this question. The church sent them on their way, and as they travelled through Phoenicia and Samaria, they told how the Gentiles had been converted. This news made all the brothers very glad. When they came to Jerusalem, they were welcomed by the church and the apostles and elders, to whom they reported everything God had done through them.

Then some of the believers who belonged to the party of the Pharisees stood up and said, 'The Gentiles must be circumcised and required to obey the law of Moses.'

The apostles and elders met to consider this question. After much discussion, Peter got up and addressed them: 'Brothers, you know that some time ago God made a choice among you that the Gentiles might hear from my lips the message of the gospel and believe. God, who knows the heart, showed that he accepted them by giving the Holy Spirit to them, just as he did to us. He made no distinction between us and them, for he purified their hearts by faith. Now then, why do you try to test God by putting on the necks of the disciples a yoke that neither we nor our fathers have been able to bear? No! We believe it is through the grace of our Lord Jesus that we are saved, just as they are.'

The whole assembly became silent as they listened to Barnabas and Paul telling about the miraculous signs and wonders God had done among the Gentiles through them. When they finished, James spoke up: 'Brothers, listen to me. Simon has described to us how God at first showed his concern by taking from the Gentiles a people for himself. The words of the prophets are in agreement with this, as it is written:

> After this I will return
>   and rebuild David's fallen tent.
> Its ruins I will rebuild,
>   and I will restore it,
> that the remnant of men may seek the Lord,
>   and all the Gentiles who bear my name,
> says the Lord, who does these things'
>   that have been known for ages.

'It is my judgment, therefore, that we should not make it difficult for the Gentiles who are turning to God. Instead we should write to them, telling them to abstain from food polluted by idols, from sexual immorality, from the meat of strangled animals and from blood. For Moses has been preached in every city from the earliest times and is read in the synagogues on every Sabbath.'

Then the apostles and elders, with the whole church, decided to choose some of their own men and send them to Antioch with Paul and Barnabas. They chose Judas (called Barsabbas) and Silas, two men who were leaders among the brothers. With them they sent the following letter:

The apostles and elders, your brothers,

To the Gentile believers in Antioch, Syria and Cilicia: Greetings.

We have heard that some went out from us without our authorisation and disturbed you, troubling your minds by what they said. So we all agreed to choose some men and send them to you with our dear friends Barnabas and Paul – men who have risked their lives for the name of our Lord Jesus Christ. Therefore we are sending Judas and Silas to confirm by word of mouth what we are writing. It seemed good to the Holy Spirit and to us not to burden you with anything beyond the following requirements: You are to abstain from food sacrificed to idols, from blood, from the meat of strangled animals and from sexual immorality. You will do well to avoid these things. Farewell.

The men were sent off and went down to Antioch, where they gathered the church together and delivered the letter. The people read it and were glad for its encouraging message. Judas and Silas, who themselves were prophets, said much to encourage and strengthen the brothers. After spending some time there, they were sent off by the brothers with the blessing of peace to return to those who had sent them. But Paul and Barnabas remained in Antioch, where they and many others taught and preached the word of the Lord.

13 Other Special Groups

From marriage to missions, from men to music

There's a bereavement support group, a group for those with learning difficulties and another for physically disabled, several practical work teams, a newcomers small group, a soup run team and a homelessness team, and . . . the list goes on. David Beer, in his book *Communication that Connects* published by Kingsway, describes some of the varied groups in his church. There can be all sorts of different small groups within a church. This chapter contains a mix of ideas with some brief outlines for all sorts of different groups. If you are using this chapter in a training course, then simply pick and mix from the different sections in order to cover the ones you are interested in.

Men's groups

Don't get locked into stereotypes. Not all men like sport. Not all men hate cooking or flower arranging. I know a guy who's an expert embroiderer – a skill he learned to while away off duty hours in the Navy. However, there are a number of topics which men are more likely to find interesting and which can be used in small groups for men.

For biblical material with a male interest try:

- Nehemiah – taking on a task and being focussed until it was achieved.
- David – very macho! But with weaknesses. A study on the life of David throws up a whole package of issues for men to explore.
- Paul – another very focussed man. Explore the lengths to which he was prepared to go in order to be obedient 'to the heavenly vision'.
- And don't forget the life of Jesus.

Men's groups – GROUP FOCUS   Ask the group to draw up their all-time great team. It could be football, cricket, rugby, athletics – whatever is topical at the time. Discuss:

- What makes a great sportsperson?
- What has to be given up to achieve greatness in sport?
- What are the rewards of great sporting achievement?

Before the session, have someone do some research about the athletics games in New Testament times and report their findings to the group.

Read Hebrews 12:1–3 and Philippians 3:12–14 and discuss:

- What needs to be given up if we are to run the race?
- How do we keep going when the going is tough?
- How do we win the prize?
- What is the prize we win?

Together plan a spiritual training programme that would equip the group to run better.

Parent and toddler group   Focus on issues like parenting which are of obvious concern, but be careful not to set too idealistic a standard and create unnecessary feelings of guilt in parents who are less than supermums or superdads.

Spend time looking at books for young children, both Christian and secular. Discuss what's popular with different children. Think through issues like whether children should be allowed books which feature magic, fairies etc.

Use creative ways of praying together (see chapter 5), especially praying for one another and the struggles of bringing up children.

Parent and toddler group – GROUP FOCUS   Brainstorm the different stages children go through from babyhood to adulthood. List them in order down one side of a sheet of paper. Opposite them list any parallels you can think of in spiritual development. Then ask group members to identify where they are in their own spiritual development. Or use the chart below to achieve the same end. (Participants on the training course can use their copy of this book. When using the technique in another group create the chart on a computer and provide copies to members.)

Where am I spiritually?

newborn	I haven't been a Christian long and I've so much to learn.
toddler	I've made progress but I'm still finding my feet.
child	I'm so curious to find out more.
teenager	I like people to think I know it all but underneath I still have a lot of questions.
parent	I have lots of responsibilities and sometimes I don't know how I'll cope.
Or	

Read Hosea 11. How do I feel when my children are naughty? How will I feel when they let me down really badly? How does God feel about us when we fail him? How can we learn to grow up as God's children? How can we support one another? Pray in pairs for each other and each other's children.

Bereavement group   Some of the prayer and worship ideas (see chapters 5 and 6) which focus on silence and reflection will be helpful. Don't be too concerned to fill the group with speech.

Bereavement group – GROUP FOCUS   One question consistently asked by the bereaved is 'Why?' Explore that question together, writing the word WHY? on a sheet of paper as large as you can and use it as a central focus for brainstorming.

Read John 11:1–44. Why:

- did Lazarus have to die?
- didn't Jesus go immediately and heal him?
- did Mary and Martha have to go through the grieving experience?
- did Martha seem to have an answer to her loss (verses 21–27)?
- was Mary angry with Jesus (verse 32)?
- did Jesus weep – after all, he knew he was going to raise Lazarus?
- was Lazarus raised only to die again at some point?
- do we hate and fear death even if it means going to heaven?

There are no precise answers to any of these questions. Simply allow the group in discussion to raise the issues. After the discussion, read aloud Revelation 21:1–4 (or use a cassette of Scripture) and leave time – perhaps with background music – for silent reflection.

Change the mood – but not too abruptly – by moving into the routine of having coffee together and letting conversation continue informally.

Women's groups   I'm thinking here of the traditional ladies' group, perhaps flourishing in the past but now reduced to quite a small number of rather elderly ladies. Encourage them to see the virtues of being a small group and gently introduce some small group techniques in place of the traditional hymn/prayer/talk sandwich.

Women's groups – GROUP FOCUS   Ask the group to share advice:

- they were given by their parents
- they have given to their children (or nephews or nieces)
- they would want to give to children today

Read together almost any chapter of Proverbs. (Chapters 16 or 25 have some interesting proverbs to provoke comment.) Or go through the book beforehand and select individual verses which you feel will be of interest. After reading the chapter, ask each person to choose just one proverb and say why they think it's important.

Choose proverbs which would be encouraging and helpful to various people in the church – such as the minister, a Sunday School teacher, youth leader, organist or musician.

Create cards featuring the proverb which can be given away appropriately. These can be as creative as the group is able: using calligraphy, embroidery, painting, or any other craft technique. This part may be an ongoing project over several weeks.

Marriage preparation – GROUP FOCUS   Try the Bible study printed at the end of this chapter with a small group of couples preparing for marriage or couples in a marriage enrichment course. The poem from Proverbs 31:10–31 may reflect a different view of the roles of husbands and wives from ours today, but it can provoke important questions about a relationship. In the training course, participants can mark their copies of this book. (It may be helpful to enlarge to A3 size.) When using the idea in your own groups you can easily create something similar on a computer. Talk through the questions, letting a different person pick the next one each time, rather than predictably working through the questions in order.

Music groups and choirs   These groups may play a prominent part in leading worship week by week. It's helpful if part of their practice time focuses on the scriptural principles underlying what they're doing. The Group Focus materials in chapters 5 and 6 would be useful here.

Another helpful practice is to take a song or hymn and look carefully at its content:

- What is the writer trying to say?
- What mood is the writer trying to create?
- Does the tune and the arrangement help the writer's purposes?
- How do we as musicians and singers use this to help us worship?
- How do we play/sing it so as to help the congregation use it to worship?

Music groups and choirs – GROUP FOCUS   Read 1 Chronicles 25:1–31. (You can skip the names!)

- verse 1: Does our music have a prophetic role in worship? How could that happen? Would it be a good thing? Is there more to music and singing than just filling in the gaps in the services and giving people an opportunity to stand up?
- verses 6,7: Who, in our church, is responsible for the supervision of musicians and singers – practically? And spiritually? And pastorally? How can we make their life easier? What can they do for us?
- verse 8: David included all ages and abilities. How do we decide who can or can't lead worship? Do we need to make any changes? How do we train new singers and musicians?

Mission groups   Do you have missionary meetings to which only the keenest of the keen come along? Try putting a mission focus into your small group system from time to time.

Have a mission focus evening which majors on a particular country or area of the world. Try:

- bringing food to eat from that country
- bringing newspaper cuttings relating to the country
- dressing in local costume
- bring news of mission work (especially individuals or organisations known to the church)
- use email or get on the phone to someone in that

country during the group session – but don't forget to check on time differences!

Mission groups – GROUP FOCUS   This is a group study to help members explore the huge range of mission going on all around them.

Read Acts 1:1–11. On a large sheet of paper draw three concentric circles. In the inner circle (Jerusalem) group members write down as many *local* mission initiatives as they can think of. Include organisations and individuals. What about church members who have a mission field at work or at school? In the second (Judaea) write down *national* initiatives. Don't forget youth camps, university missions etc. In the third (ends of the earth) write *international* ones. When you have filled the circles, praise God that so much is going on. Highlight with coloured pens those the church is directly involved with, or supports financially or in other ways. Split into twos and threes and pray for initiatives in the circles.

Resources

50 Outlines for Men's Meetings Dave Roberts and Howard Lewis. Kingsway. Discussion-based topics for men's groups.

100 Talks for Parents Fiona Castle and Joyce Gledhill. Kingsway. Talk outlines for use in parent and toddler groups.

77 Bible Studies for 21st Century Mums Mary Pytches. Monarch. Ten-minute messages for mums in coffee mornings, playgroups etc.

Communication That Connects   David Beer. Kingsway.

Reflect

Do I want to see all sorts of groups in the church functioning in the best way or do I feel it's easier just to let things run as they've always done?

Takeaway

Which small groups in my church could most benefit from introducing new ideas?

MARRIAGE PREPARATION GROUP

How do we develop confidence in each other?

What skills do I bring to this relationship?

Who will be earning and who will be spending? How will we balance the books?

How will our partnership enrich us – how will it enrich others?

Are clothes and possessions a big issue for us?

Will both of us go out to work?

What are our strengths – and our weaknesses?

Do we want children? How many? When?

Are we able to give and receive compliments and praise?

Is God in our relationship?

A wife of noble character who can find?
    She is worth far more than rubies.
Her husband has full confidence in her
    and lacks nothing of value.
She brings him good, not harm,
    all the days of her life.
She selects wool and flax
    and works with eager hands.
She is like the merchant ships
    bringing her food from afar.
She gets up while it is still dark;
    she provides food for her family
    and portions for her servant girls.
She considers a field and buys it;
    out of her earnings she plants a vineyard.
She sets about her work vigorously;
    her arms are strong for her tasks.
She sees that her trading is profitable,
    and her lamp does not go out at night.
In her hand she holds the distaff
    and grasps the spindle with her fingers.
She opens her arms to the poor
    and extends her hands to the needy.
When it snows, she has no fear for her
        household;
    for all of them are clothed in scarlet.
She makes coverings for her bed;
    she is clothed in fine linen and purple.
Her husband is respected at the city gate,
    where he takes his seat among the elders of
        the land.
She makes linen garments and sells them,
    and supplies the merchants with sashes.
She is clothed with strength and dignity;
    she can laugh at the days to come.
She speaks with wisdom,
    and faithful instruction is on her tongue.
She watches over the affairs of her
        household
    and does not eat the bread of idleness.
Her children arise and call her blessed;
    her husband also, and he praises her:
'Many women do noble things,
    but you surpass them all.'
Charm is deceptive, and beauty is fleeting;
    but a woman who fears the Lord is to be
        praised.
Give her the reward she has earned,
    and let her works bring her praise at the
        city gate.

Proverbs 31:10–31

How do we protect each other from harm? How do we 'bring good' to one another?

Who's going to do the shopping . . . and the cooking?

What are our strengths?

Will we have enough to live on?

How will other people see us?

What if one of us earns more than the other?

Will we be faithful?

Do we tend to be lazy?

Do we see each other as we really are?

Do we say 'I love you' often enough?

14 Moving On

Encouraging growth and managing change

When small groups work well, group members build strong friendships and can be reluctant to see the group split or changed. Expectation of change needs to be built into the group from the beginning. If the empty chair principle (see chapter 9) is encouraged, then groups will be changing by the regular addition of new members. This means that at some point a small group will no longer be small. I suggest that when a group gets to about 16 members it is time to split. If not all members are attending regularly then it might be advisable to wait until the group reaches 20. It is important that the two new groups being formed have sufficient regulars to be viable. One of the most depressing aspects of small group life is when only two or three people turn up for the group and the whole group dynamic is changed.

These important principles should be established from the beginning:

- All small group leaders should know and support the strategy that small groups are intended to draw new members in, grow, and split so that the total number of groups multiplies.
- Group leaders should encourage their groups to see growth as normal, and splitting into two groups as a goal to be achieved.
- Continually train new group leaders. In an ideal world each small group will have a trainee leader being prepared to take over the new group.

Work towards change together Splitting the group should not be imposed from outside but should be something the group works towards. Here are the steps:

- When the group gets to around 12 to 14, start planning the strategy for the new group. Where will it meet? Who will move out to form it?
- Start to pray for new members to join the group so that it will become large enough to split.
- When the group is about to split into two, organise a celebration meal or some other special event.
- Make sure everyone in each of the two groups has the phone numbers and email addresses of people in the other group.
- Keep information flowing between the two groups so that each group can pray for the other.
- In the first year of the two new groups arrange occasional events at which both groups can meet together.

At various times it may be necessary for individuals to move to a different group. This might be because they go to lead another group, because another group is too small and needs an infusion of members or because someone just doesn't feel at home in their group and wants to try another. Whatever the reason, mark the move with some sort of farewell and prayer and keep in touch for some period of time.

Too few to continue What about when a group is not growing but rather falling in numbers and reaches the point where it is no longer viable? Here's a plan of action:

- Do something before the group reaches such small numbers that every meeting becomes a gloomy and disappointing experience.
- Consider the reasons for the group's failure to thrive. This should be done initially by those leaders responsible for the overall small group strategy in the church and then discussed with the small group leader and finally with the group itself.
- Three strategies may be considered. 1: Is it possible to make a special effort to recruit new members? 2: Can new members be brought in from other groups? 3: Should the group be closed and members asked to join other groups?
- If the group is to be closed, do not major on the problems which have caused this. Celebrate the history of the group and pray for individual members as they move into other groups. It is probably not wise in this situation for all the members of the closed group to move en bloc to another group. Encourage them to share themselves out among several groups.

Ideas

Produce a map of your town, city or village with the location of the small groups marked on it. Also mark areas where you would like to see small groups established.

Give groups opportunities to share encouragements and prayer requests with the wider church, perhaps as part of Sunday worship or on special occasions when all the groups are brought together.

GROUP FOCUS

On the maps on the **Moving on . . .** page at the end of this chapter ask everyone to plot the major geographical moves they have made in their lives (not including holidays). Some people may have lived all their lives in the same place. Some may only have moved around this country. Some may have moved around the world. When completed, each person finds a partner and shares their journeys.

In the whole group, talk about the fears that moving on

brings. How much of the fear turned out to be justified and how much not?

Read Genesis 12:1–9. Imagine yourself in the position of Abraham.

- What would you miss most in your old life?
- What would you fear most in your new life?
- What would be your incentive for moving?

How do we know when God is calling us to move?
Read Numbers 14:1–9. Discuss together:

- If you had been among the Israelites, what would have been your fears about going into Canaan?
- Which is better? To be badly off in a place you know? Or to face the future in an unknown place (verse 4)?
- What did this generation of people lose by their fear of moving on?

Think about other sorts of moves we make in our lives. Again in pairs, share how you felt about these moves:

- from primary school to secondary school
- from one job to another
- from one home to another

Read Acts 8:1–8. Together make a list of the advantages which came from the Christians being scattered. In our lives what are the advantages of moving:

- to a new job?
- to a new home?
- to a new church?

What challenges does each of these present? In pairs share together your experiences of changing churches.

Read Acts 13:1–3. Imagine you are the church committee responsible for managing the church at Antioch. How many reasons can you think of why it would not be sensible, practical or appropriate for key leaders like Paul and Barnabas to leave at this particular time? ('Paul's one of our best preachers. Numbers at services will fall if he's not speaking.') How do we balance the challenge of sending people out into new work against the needs of those who remain behind?

Read 2 Timothy 2:1–7. Split the group into three. Bearing in mind what Paul writes about in this passage, each group is to write a letter to one of the people below (assuming you know them pretty well) offering advice and guidance.

- A small group leader who doesn't want a deputy and never allows anyone else to take any responsibility.
- A group member who says 'I like it where I am. I get on with the people. I don't want anything to change.'
- A member who says 'Getting involved with another group is too much like hard work. I want an easy life.'

Read the letters aloud to the whole group. Spend some time in prayer about real life situations (in the group or known to the group) which involve moving on.

Reflecting on all you've covered in this study, either draw up a simple leaflet entitled 'Ten Reasons for Moving On' which could be given to small group members at the time when the group is splitting and moving on; or create a series of slogans and images for an advertising campaign based on the idea that moving on is good for individuals, good for the church and good for the kingdom.

Review

Group members were asked to share a number of instances of 'moving on' in their lives. Did this help to earth the discussion in real life experiences? How helpful was the map in giving a focus for the first sharing of experiences? How does letter writing or writing a leaflet compare with straightforward discussion in helping people work through the issues?

Resources

Change Directions David Cormack. Monarch.
The Small Group Leader John Mallinson. Scripture Union. This has an excellent chapter on terminating (either closing or dividing) a group.

To think about . . .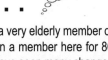

A visiting dignitary was introduced to a very elderly member of the church. 'I understand you've been a member here for 80 years,' said the dignitary. 'You must have seen many changes in that time.' 'Yes,' the church member replied. 'And I've opposed every one of them.'

Reflect

How well do I cope with change? What factors have helped me adjust to new situations?

Takeaway

What have been my past experiences of changing groups, or observing others change groups? What are the positives and what are the negatives? What key principles need to be taken on board for managing change more effectively?

Diary

Month 1 – Why my group? And why me? I don't want to move. I'm happy where I am. What's the point of making friendships and getting used to each other if it's all going to change?

Month 2 – Well, at least the new group is easier to get to. Only positive thing I can say about it though.

Month 3 – They want us to have a joint meeting with our old group next week. Can't think why. Things are going really well in our new group. Perhaps the ones we left behind aren't coping too well without us?

Moving on ...

15 Troubleshooting for Groups

Identifying and handling problems creatively

You've probably heard this one. A voice comes from the bedroom. 'I won't get up. I don't want to go to school. Why should I?' From the kitchen comes the reply. 'Because it's Monday morning, you're 45 years old, and you're the head teacher!'

Sometimes leaders just don't want to lead. When you feel it's all too much for you, try to analyse the reasons:

Too pressured   Other areas of your life may be stressful. If work is tough and/or there are problems at home and/or . . . then even areas where there seems to be no pressure will be affected too.

Too tired   Check out how much sleep you're getting. A new baby at home keeping you awake every night may be the simple explanation as to why you can't concentrate on the Bible or get into prayer as well as you could.

Not enough input   Are you missing church services or leaders' preparation meetings? Has your own study and prayer time slackened off? We can go so far on 'reserve' but eventually if we're not taking in we won't be able to give out.

Doing too much   I know what it's like to be part of a small church where everyone has several jobs to do. But it's very easy to take on one job too many.

Problems within the group   Your lack of enthusiasm may be caused by problems within the group. We'll look at some of those in a moment.

Reflect

Do I recognise myself in any of the above scenarios? Can I identify any other reasons why my enthusiasm has waned?

Tackling the problem   Once you've diagnosed the problem, what can you do about it? You may be able to tackle the root problem; give up another job you're doing at church; get stuck in to a course of study. But often the root problem cannot be immediately sorted; the problems at work won't go away; the baby won't stop crying. Here are some suggestions:

- Find people you can trust to pray for you and/or with you. Ask them to pray for the root problem and for the energy and enthusiasm needed to run the group.
- Talk the situation over with a minister or someone else you trust who may be able to see solutions from outside that you, on the inside, cannot see.
- Look at the possibility of sharing responsibility. We looked at the issue of training others to lead in the last chapter. Is there someone in the group who could take more responsibility?

- What about taking a break? Can you hand over the group to someone else for three months, six months or whatever?
- Perhaps the time is right to give up leading the group altogether. Although it's not a good thing to give up responsibilities every time we feel a bit down, there comes a time when the pressure of doing a job is so great that for our own sake and for the sake of others we should give it up. This is not failure – it is simply a recognition that God does not call us into jobs for life and that none of us is indispensable.

Reflect

Where does my support and encouragement come from?

Problems in the group   We looked briefly at some issues of group dynamics (how people relate together) in chapter 2. It might be helpful to read that through again. But, assuming you've got the basics right, how do you deal with:

The talkative   Where one person dominates the meeting it might be helpful to speak to them privately along the lines of 'It's really great, the way you're always ready to contribute to the discussion and I know you've got a lot of good things to say. I'd like you to help me even more. I'm worried that some of the shyer members of the group aren't joining in, so I'd like you to make a special effort to hold back and let other people speak before you share your thoughts.' You may need to interrupt this person on occasions to reinforce the message: 'Hold on a minute; I'm sure you've got something good to say, but let's hear from some others first.'

The shy   Some people don't join in because they can't cope with the flow of discussion and find an opening to speak. If you have someone you know has things to share but doesn't seem to get into the discussion, then specifically ask them for a comment to give them an opportunity to speak. If someone is not speaking because they don't have anything to say, then look at the kinds of questions you're asking and the subjects you're discussing. There should always be questions anyone could answer: 'How would you feel in that situation?' 'Have you ever been in a situation where you've had to make a difficult decision?' and so on.

The wacky and the obsessed   I'm talking about the kind of people who always take the discussion off on a totally different track, either because they are the kind of people who make mental leaps unintelligible to the rest, or because they always want to bring everything round to their pet topic. Make a decision as to how often and how long you're going to allow these people to speak. Then be ruthless in bringing the discussion back on track.

The gossip Nothing destroys the freedom of a group to share their needs and cares more than the knowledge that what they say is going to be all round the church by next Sunday! Inside the group stress the need for confidentiality. Outside the group, if necessary, speak firmly but lovingly to the person concerned.

The mix Make sure there are opportunities for everyone to get to know everyone else. When splitting into pairs for prayer or discussion make sure people move around so that everyone talks and prays with everyone else. Encourage patience and tolerance – groups take a while to begin to function smoothly. But where it is impossible to integrate someone, prayerfully consider the possibility that they need to move to a different group.

Bigger problems Sometimes the group gets out of step or even seriously at odds with the church leadership or the rest of the church, creating the potential for a split. In this situation the leader needs to:

- Keep clear lines of communication with church leaders. Without relaying comments of individual members, church leaders should be kept aware of grievance within the group.
- Act early. Try to resolve problems and misunderstandings before they become too big.
- Try to be detached. If the group leader is caught up in the feelings of the group then judgement is likely to be clouded.
- Try to focus the group on listening to God. If a group is genuinely prepared to pray about painful issues and to listen for an answer from God then surprising results can ensue.

Sometimes a group feels badly let down by one of its members, or you as leader, or someone outside the group. Work this through:

- Without being pious and unrealistic, focus on the importance of forgiveness and reconciliation.
- Don't just say 'you must forgive so and so' but help the group work through the issues together and with God so that they can come to the point of forgiveness on their own initiative.
- Be ready to admit your own faults and failings.
- Don't join in criticisms of others – however justified they may seem to be.
- Keep praying!

GROUP FOCUS

Ask members of the group to share situations where they have been involved in an argument (nothing too recent which might still be painful). How was the argument resolved? What would they have done differently with hindsight?

Read Acts 15:36–41 and 13:13. Divide the group into three. One group prepares Paul's arguments for not taking Mark. One group prepares Barnabas' arguments for taking Mark. One group prepares Mark's explanation of events (some imagination needed here). Present the three cases, then together consider whether there was any other way in which the situation could have been resolved? Read 2 Timothy 4:11 to see the end of the story.

Discuss together the best way to handle people who:

- only come to the group when they feel like it
- promise to do things and then don't
- always disagree with decisions
- break confidences

Add in any other issues you feel are likely to occur.

Read 1 Timothy 5:1,2. If you have representatives of Paul's four groups (older men, younger men, older women, younger women) in your group, ask them to share how they feel when they are challenged about something they've said or done. If not all are represented, the group must try to put themselves in those positions. Does it make any difference whether the leader who challenges them is:

- younger?
- older?
- same sex?
- different sex?
- someone close?
- someone distant?

What implications do Paul's instructions about 'absolute purity' have for leaders?

Play a game in which one person makes a statement. The person next to them has to make a statement contradicting the first. Then the next different statement contradicts the second and so on until people run out of steam. Then read 2 Timothy 2:14–16, 22–26 and discuss the following:

- What are the main causes of quarrels in church life?
- How can they best be avoided?
- What can leaders do to reconcile people in dispute?
- Is it always wrong to disagree with someone? Look at Galatians 2:11–14. How do we discuss, debate and even disagree without quarrelling?

Read Matthew 5:3–10 and turn these Beatitudes into prayers for yourself and for other members of the group.

To think about . . .

'The value and richness of the group's life and the individual's own spiritual growth will come, in part, out of coping with and loving people who think differently.' Jon Bush in *Housegroups* Ed. Ian Coffey & Stephen Gaukroger. IVP

Resources

The Sheep That Got Away   Michael J Fanstone. Monarch. Based on surveys in 1991. Looks at why people leave the church.

A Churchless Faith   Alan Jamieson. SPCK. Fascinating and challenging book about the lessons to be learned from those who have left evangelical, Pentecostal and charismatic churches but nevertheless continued their journey of faith.

Conflict   Pauline Bell and Pauline Jordan. Scripture Union. A practical guide to handling conflict in the church. Out of print but copies available from Christian Resources Project, 14 Lipson Road, Plymouth, PL4 8PW.

Reflect

Am I still struggling with hurts I've received in previous church quarrels? Do I need to talk issues through with someone? Do I want to be a peacemaker?

Takeaway

Is my group peaceful but boring? Active, always involved in something – but not all of it positive? A pretty good balance of life and love? What are my key objectives for dealing with things that are wrong and preventing things from going wrong?

Bible passages and study methods

Chapter	Bible verses	Study method
1	Joshua 1:1–9 Matthew 23 John 13:1–17 1 Timothy 3:1–12	listing qualities of leadership
	1, 2 Timothy	analysing teaching on leadership by making mini books
2	Matthew	board game
3	Luke 15	dramatic reading, acting, devising questions
	2 Timothy 3:14–17	listing and relating to other Bible passages and life situations
4		research to find Bible teaching on controversial topic
5	Matthew 6:5–18	using Lord's Prayer as a pattern for prayer
	Paul's prayers	analysing prayer topics and applying to our prayer life
6	1 Corinthians 14:26–40	discovering guidelines for participation in group meetings
7	Philippians 2:1–18	brainstorming; analysing qualities of Christ-like life
	1 Corinthians 13:4–7	creating problems and solutions to illustrate description of love
8	Various	pastoral care scenarios
9	John 1:35–51	discovering who we can invite and devising invitations
	Hebrews 13:2 and other passages	exploring examples of entertaining angels; researching the occurrence of strangers in the Bible
10	Acts 17:16–34	creating a non-Christian creed; talking through the passage
11	Proverbs 17:6	selecting answers from sheet
	1 John 2:9–17	exploring occurrences of 'children' in 1 John
12	Acts 13:1–3	discussion
	Acts 15:1–35	underlining and making margin notes
	Acts 6:1–7	drawing up job descriptions
13	Hebrews 12:1–3 Philippians 3:12–14	sporting greatness and athletic analogies
	Hosea 1	exploring feelings about our children
	John 11:1–44	'why' questions
	Proverbs	exploring traditional wisdom and sending proverb cards
	Proverbs 31:10–31	questions around the text
	1 Chronicles 25	discussion
	Acts 1:1–11	brainstorming on paper
14	Genesis 12:1–9 Numbers 14:1–9 Acts 8:1–8 Acts 13:1–3	using maps and life experiences to explore the issues around moving on
	2 Timothy 2:1–7	writing letters to deal with specific issues
15	Acts 15:36–41; 13:13	role playing Paul, Barnabas and Mark
	1 Timothy 5:1, 2	exploring reactions of different age groups
	Matthew 5:3–10	turning the Beatitudes into prayer

Afterword

When you've completed the training don't throw this book away!

- Use the table of Scripture passages for inspiration when you're looking for ideas for dealing with different parts of the Bible. Use the methods we've used on different passages.
- Keep going back to the **Ideas** sections to try something new. And keep on creating your own extra ideas in a supplementary list or file.
- Set yourself the task of reading at least some of the books that have been recommended.

Have a great time with your group! And, hopefully, grow your church – and God's glorious kingdom – in the process!

Mike Law
January 2003

Resources for Small Groups from Scripture Union

CONNECT BIBLE STUDIES

Innovative thought-provoking group Bible studies exploring key issues raised by popular contemporary films, TV programmes, books and music. Four weeks of material in each. Also available online: www.connectbiblestudies.com

£3.00
Harry Potter   1 85999 578 0
The Matrix   1 85999 579 9
All that you can't leave behind / U2   1 85999 580 2
Billy Elliot   1 85999 581 0
Chocolat   1 85999 608 6
TV Game Shows   1 85999 609 4
How to be Good   1 85999 610 8
Destiny's Child: 'Survivor'   1 85999 613 2
AI: Artificial Intelligence   1 85999 626 4
Lord of the Rings   1 85999 634 5
The Simpsons   1 85999 529 2
Iris   1 85999 669 8
Dido: No Angel   1 85999 679 5
On Football   1 85999 690 6
Superheroes   1 85999 702 3
The Pullman Trilogy   1 85999 714 7
And more titles following.

BODYBUILDERS

A highly relational small group resource that's flexible and fun to use. Six outlines in each booklet contain notes for leaders, prayer and worship ideas, photocopiable sheets of interactive and in-depth Bible study material and ideas for personal study during the week.

£3.50
A Fresh Encounter   David Bolster   1 85999 586 1
Designed for Great Things   Anton Baumohl   1 85999 585 3
Living for the King   'Tricia Williams   1 85999 584 5
Relationship Building   Lance Pierson   1 85999 582 9
Surviving Under Pressure   Christopher Griffiths & Stephen Hathway   1 85999 587 X
Growing Through Change   Lance Pierson   1 85999 583 7

EQUIPPED FOR LIVING

Four booklets designed for Christians wanting in-depth Bible study in an engaging, personal style. Thought-provoking questions for personal reflection and application to life as well as for group discussion. Between eight and ten studies in each book. By Florence MacKenzie, illustrated by quotes from a wide variety of authors.

£3.50
Living out the life of Jesus: The Fruit of the Spirit   1 85999 430 X
Living the kingdom lifestyle: The Beatitudes   1 85999 460 1
Living empowered for ministry: The Gifts of the Spirit   1 85999 458 X
Living under God's protection: The Armour of God   1 85999 450 4

CHRISTIAN LIFE AND WORK

Stressed at the office, factory or shop? The only Christian in your workplace? From Scripture Union and London Bible College comes a video-based small group package to help you explore living out your faith. Includes video, leader's workbook and a copy of Mark Greene's best-selling book *Thank God It's Monday*.

Package £25.00
1 85999 532 2
Book only £5.99
1 85999 503 9

CHRISTIAN LIFE AND TODAY'S WORLD

How can we take up the challenge of living as Christians in a postmodern society? Also from Scripture Union and London Bible College is this stimulating small group resource containing video, accompanying workbook for group leaders and book of articles written by members of the LBC faculty.

Package £25.00
1 85999 576 4
Book only £5.99
1 85999 560 8

All these resources and more from SU available from your local Christian bookshop.

For a free catalogue giving details of the full range of resources for small groups:

- phone Scripture Union's mail order line: 01908 856006
- email info@scriptureunion.org.uk
- fax 01908 856020
- log on to www.Scriptureunion.org.uk
- write to SU Mail Order, PO Box 5148, Milton Keynes MLO, MK2 2YX

SCRIPTURE UNION

USING THE BIBLE TO INSPIRE CHILDREN, YOUNG PEOPLE AND ADULTS TO KNOW GOD